WOMEN'S VOICES
from
LATIN AMERICA

Evelyn Picon Garfield

WOMEN'S VOICES
from
LATIN
AMERICA

Interviews with Six Contemporary Authors

WAYNE STATE UNIVERSITY PRESS   DETROIT 1987

91 90 89 88 87   1 2 3 4 5

Library of Congress Cataloging-in-Publication Data

Women's voices from Latin America.

Bibliography: p.
1. Spanish American fiction—Women authors—
History and criticism.   2. Spanish American fiction—
20th century—History and criticism.   3. Novelists,
Spanish American—20th century—Interviews.
I. Garfield, Evelyn Picon.
[PQ7082.N7W66 1987]   863'.009'9287   87–25354
ISBN 0–8143–1962–9 (pbk. : alk. paper)

To my mother,
Edith Haskell Picon,
with love

Ah, Dolores! The brief time we spent together isn't important. The intensity is what counts, the world we glimpsed, the fear we shared. And I don't mind telling you that my hands are perpetually frozen and that they'd gladly reach out to you for warmth. Let's take things one at a time, sister; let's see if we create or are mere witnesses.

Marta Traba,
Conversación al sur

And I tried to remember any case in the course of my reading where two women are represented as friends. There is an attempt at it in Diana of the Crossways. *They are confidantes, of course, in Racine and the Greek tragedies. They are now and then mothers and daughters. But almost without exception they are shown in their relation to men.*

Virginia Woolf,
A Room of One's Own

CONTENTS

(*Left to right*) Gabriela Mistral, Alfonsina Storni, and Juana de Ibarbourou. (Photo from archive of Manuel Pedro González.)

PREFACE

EARLY IN THE SEVENTIES, the Mexican writer and critic Margo Glantz sent me two volumes of short stories by the contemporary Uruguayan Armonía Somers. Up until then, my acquaintance with fiction by Latin American women authors had been limited, circumscribed by their minimal representation in literary anthologies and in American university course offerings in which Latin America is studied. Even specialists in Latin American culture and letters at that time rarely paid attention to works by female authors, with the exception of the women poets from the Southern Cone—Uruguay, Argentina, Chile—such as Gabriela Mistral, Alfonsina Storni, Delmira Agustini, and Juana de Ibarbourou.

The quality of Somers's short stories motivated me to question how many other works of this high caliber written by women remained relatively unknown even to Hispanists in the United States. I consulted numerous anthologies of literary selections of and critical essays (in Spanish) on contemporary Spanish American letters, including those edited by Enrique Anderson Imbert and Eugenio Florit, Carlos Fuen-

11

tes, Julio Ortega, Emir Rodríguez Monegal, Juan Loveluck, Luis Harss and Barbara Dohmann, and Rita Guibert.[1] The virtual absence of information about Latin American women authors and their work in those anthologies, led me to conclude that the relative ignorance of the literary production of these women was due, at least in part, to their insufficient representation in anthologies of Spanish American literature utilized in this country, to the poor distribution of books by Latin American publishers in foreign markets, and to the paucity of critical material on female prose writers in literary journals.

I decided, therefore, to focus my investigation on prose writers rather than on poets, for the latter had received more attention in the past. In addition, in the initial stages of my research, I was influenced by the international fascination with contemporary authors of the so-called "boom" years (the second half of the 1960s), during which period some Latin American male authors saw their fiction increasingly translated and published abroad. To my knowledge, contemporary women authors had not yet been similarly acknowledged, and I intended to discover whether or not some of them might also merit recognition beyond their national boundaries.

I had barely begun my research on novels, short stories, and drama in the original Spanish and Portuguese when I realized how considerable the body of creative works by Latin American women really was. I found myself forced to select a few authors from among the most masterful artists whose narratives, in my opinion, were of significant literary value to warrant a more profound and thorough investigation: Julieta Campos, Marta Traba, Luisa Valenzuela, Griselda Gambaro, Elvira Orphée, Armonía Somers, and Clarice Lispector. I was convinced that their works merited more than the acclaim and awards received in their homelands. To fill the critical void, I published articles about these women in Spanish and simultaneously searched for English translations of their fiction and criticism about them in English in order to assure their accessibility to non-Spanish readers in the United States.

The search was in vain. Early in the forties and fifties, some of the novels by women from the early twentieth century, like María Luisa Bombal (Chile) and Teresa de la Parra (Venezuela) were published in English in limited editions,[2] now out of print. In the mid-1970s, fiction by women from Latin America was only occasionally translated: a short story by Armonía Somers or a play by Griselda Gambaro; Clarice Lispector's *The Apple in the Dark* and her collection of short stories *Family Ties;* Luisa Valenzuela's *Clara.*[3] Female prose writers have not fared better in recent anthologies of Latin American literature (in English), such as those edited by Willis Knapp Jones, Anne Fremantle, Emir Rodríguez Monegal, and José Donoso and William Henkin.[4] In spite of this dearth of fiction in print, by the mid-seventies an interest in women's literature developed among students and scholars of Hispanic cultures: several doctoral dissertations were completed in English, particularly on Mexican and Argentinian women novelists, and Ann Pescatello edited a collection of studies, *Female and Male in Latin America: Essays,* which provided scholars with useful sociological information for the analysis of female roles in Latin American literature.[5]

Because resource materials were so limited in Spanish, Portuguese, and English, I decided to correspond with the seven authors whose fiction attracted my attention. My hope was to arrange interviews with them as I had previously done in 1973 with the Argentinian author Julio Cortázar in southern France.[6] On the basis of my experience with Cortázar, I was convinced that such interviews provide valuable insights into the life and works of a writer. By 1978, I had arranged for and completed interviews with the six authors featured in this anthology (the seventh, Clarice Lispector, died in 1977 before my arrival in Brazil).

In the early eighties, interest in Latin American women authors burgeoned, and many of their works were translated into English. For example, selections by new poets appeared in the anthology *Open to the Sun* by Nora Jacquez Wieser; Luisa Valenzuela published *Strange Things Happen Here;* a two-volume anthology of prose and poetry translations was edited by Doris Meyer and Margarite Fernández Olmos entitled *Contemporary Women Authors of Latin America;* and scattered selections had shown up in journals as diverse as *The Center of Inter-American Relations Review, Antaeus,* and *Ms* magazine.[7] Additional research tools became available to the non-Spanish reader with the publication of such volumes as *Women Writers in Translation: An Annotated Bibliography, 1945–1980,* edited by Margery Resnick and Isabelle de Courtivron, and Meri Knaster's *Women in Spanish America: An Annotated Bibliography from Pre-Conquest to Contempo-*

rary Times.[8] Also, several international Conferences on Inter-American Women Writers were held in the United States, Canada, and Mexico. And the historian Asunción Lavrin compiled a collection of essays about Latin American women which included a chapter on the feminist press in nineteenth-century Brazil.[9]

It was not difficult to link the increased activity in the area of Latin American women authors to the growth of the women's studies movement begun in the late 1960s on university campuses in the United States. By the early 1980s women's studies programs had been organized at over 350 colleges, and at least twenty-five courses in women's studies were being offered by each of 600 other colleges. These programs had evolved to encompass several aims, among them, to enlarge the sample of what scholars study and to challenge the prevailing definition of what is worthy of scholarly interest and analysis. Perhaps the historian Carolyn C. Lougee describes these goals best in her assertion that we should perceive Western civilization as a reflection of a variety of "voices of human experience."

> Then we will be able to understand that women troubadours expressed the challenges of human life in the 13th century as well as Aquinas' Quaestios did; that accused witches groped in their confessions of guilt to understand human life just as Descartes did with his Cogito; that the French mothers of illegitimate babies wondered in their Declarations de Gossesse [*sic*] about emotion and social change as acutely as Rousseau did; that Christine de Pisan's lament ("Alas, God, why was I not born into this world as a member of the masculine sex?") expresses aspects of the human condition as poignantly as does Hamlet's "To be or not to be."[10]

Women's Voices from Latin America: Interviews with Six Contemporary Authors responds to this need for a variety of "voices of human experience." It is meant to assist the English-reading public in enlarging and enriching its knowledge of Latin American contemporary literature and culture. The result of extensive scholarly research, this volume serves as an introduction to the lives, careers, and creative expressions of six accomplished writers. Providing dialogues with them, brief critical essays about specific aspects of their fiction, and selective bio-bibliographic materials, this book is intended primarily for those women and men whose interests lie in the areas of Hispanic literatures and cultures, comparative literary studies, Latin American area studies, women's studies, sociology, history, humanities studies, creative writing, and translation of literary texts. Previous volumes of interviews (in English) with Latin American authors—*Into the Mainstream* and *Seven Voices*—have served a similar purpose with regard to a limited number of male authors, most of whom were to gain wide recognition during the "boom" years. The increased distribution of some of their books abroad and the translations of others had just begun and one of those authors, Gabriel García Márquez, received the Nobel Prize for Literature in 1982. That coveted award had been bestowed on a Latin American for the first time in 1945, when the Chilean poet Gabriela Mistral also became the first female recipient. Unfortunately, Mistral was overlooked by most U.S. reporters in the early 1980s, who selectively recalled only former Latin American Nobel prize winners like Pablo Neruda and Miguel Angel Asturias.[11]

My selection of the six authors in this book is not intended to emphasize them at the expense of many other talented writers, but rather to present a thorough picture of a limited number of outstanding authors instead of a sketchy and superficial catalogue of many. My personal preferences are based in part on these authors' skillful cultivation of diverse genres and styles as well as on the multiplicity of their perspectives on reality, all of which constitute a significant professional contribution to prose fiction within the context of contemporary Latin American letters. My choices do not in any way conform to a sample in order to prove any theory concerning Spanish American female authors in general, or vis-à-vis male authors. Nor was geographic distribution a qualitative criterion of any great weight in the selection.

Nevertheless, a historical explanation might help to clarify the apparent preponderance of Argentinians in this volume. The region that is now Argentina had shown relatively little cultural development during the colonial period in comparison to Peru or Mexico. But, at the turn of the century, Argentine society began to flourish, in part due to its development of a modern economy, immigration, and the growth of the influence of European cultures. During the first half of the twentieth century, Argentinians could take advantage of one of the best university systems in Latin America. Buenos Aires became the continent's cultural center for major presses, a successful book trade, and internationally respected periodicals like *Sur*, which in the first nineteen years of its existence (1931–50) published creative selections by

182 Latin Americans, 41 Spaniards, and over 227 authors from non-Hispanic nations.[12] *Sur* introduced Argentinians to Greene, Faulkner, Woolf, Huxley, Saroyan, Steinbeck, Whitman, Camus, Gide, Sartre, Brecht, Mann, Croce, and Rabindranath Tagore, among others. A compelling force in Latin American culture, *Sur* was founded and organized under the guidance of Victoria Ocampo, who became, in 1977, shortly before her death, the first female admitted to the Argentine Academy of Letters. Thus the cultural wealth of Buenos Aires has provided a fertile environment for the development of numerous contemporary Argentinian writers, among them four of the women interviewed for this volume.

The interviews with Luisa Valenzuela and Elvira Orphée were conducted in Buenos Aires; the former now resides in New York City. I visited with the Argentinian Marta Traba in Caracas, Venezuela, before she moved to Washington, D.C., and with her countrywoman Griselda Gambaro in Ottawa, Canada, where she had traveled from her residence in Barcelona, Spain, to attend a Conference on Inter-American Women Writers. She later returned to Argentina. In Montevideo, I dialogued with Armonía Somers and in Mexico City with Julieta Campos. Before holding each of these six interviews (all done between 1976 and 1978), I had completed the study of all the works written by these authors and reviewed their scant bibliographies available here in the United States. During my visits, the authors themselves assisted me in gathering more extensive bibliographic sources from their own files and from national libraries and presses. In 1982, I asked the authors to update the interview materials by answering questions I mailed to them. These updates are set off by an ornament at the end of each interview. The interviews were conducted in Spanish and then translated by me into English. The biographies and bibliographies are selective. Unless otherwise specified, I translated all quoted material.

ACKNOWLEDGMENTS

I WOULD LIKE TO express my warmest gratitude to Armonía Somers, Elvira Orphée, Griselda Gambaro, Julieta Campos, and Luisa Valenzuela, who so graciously gave of their time and hospitality and shared with me the many conversations that can never be duplicated faithfully on paper where the atmosphere that surrounded each author during the interviews is rendered invisible. In memory of Marta Traba, whose tragic death occurred in November of 1983, I can only phrase my gratitude in the words of her own characters: "The brief time we spent together isn't important. The intensity is what counts." To Marvin Schindler for making possible the transcription of the interview tapes, María Antonieta Olivares for the actual transcription of those interviews, and Esperanza Ordóñez for her assistance in typing the final manuscript, I express my appreciation. To Linda Gould Levine and Gloria Feiman Waldman for their pioneering interviews with women in Spain, I give my respect and admiration. I am indebted to Irene Tiersten, author and friend, for her creativity which

17

will always be a source of inspiration to me. And, finally I want to offer my heartfelt appreciation to my colleague and companion, Ivan A. Schulman, for sharing with me those years of exhilarating travel, research, and writing.

INTRODUCTION

IN RECENT DECADES, WITH the new-found popularity of contemporary Latin American fiction in translation, many commentators have erroneously categorized writers in a polarized fashion as either portrayers of the so-called "real" Latin America, like Gabriel García Márquez, or those influenced by European trends, like Jorge Luis Borges or Julio Cortázar. Such facile stereotyping fails to take into consideration the complex nature of modern literature in Third World countries where, perhaps more than elsewhere, writers, like the six authors presented here, are tied to their cultural heritage. In this volume, brief introductions to the interviews outline each author's individual accomplishments, but this introduction is intended to emphasize the writers' place within a larger framework of more than a century in Latin America's Age of Modernity. These authors can hardly be appreciated without recognizing the persistent historical roots that sustain their formation. Therefore, in this introduction, I will periodically go back in time, away from the contemporary context of these six women, to the late nineteenth century when modern Latin American societies and literature were born, and even beyond to colonial times in which we will find the seeds of some traits that still endure in Latin American fiction today.

A broad range of political, social, aesthetic, and philosophical preoccupations link these women to the "triple opposition" of the critical stance taken by writers in modern societies: opposition to tradition; opposition to bourgeois culture with its ideas based on rationalism, utility, and progress; and opposition to the artist's very own aesthetic expression as a new tradition.[1] Armonía Somers unmasks the hypocritical ethics of her society and tackles prevailing taboos about sexuality, while Luisa Valenzuela explores eroticism, and through it, the one of two strongholds of power: sex and politics. Marta Traba challenges the socioeconomic and historical status quo by exposing the frivolity of the upper middle class, the abject misery of life in the lower middle class ghetto, and the scars that mark all of society as the result of civil strife. And both Elvira Orphée and Griselda Gambaro reveal the inhumanity of men towards each other through their characters' protests against the humiliation and disillusionment created by their social and biological destinies (Orphée) and their subjugation by an authoritarian force due to their own passivity and inability to assume responsiblity for their own freedom (Gambaro).

In modern Latin American societies these critical oppositions to traditional modes of behavior can be traced historically to a few rebellious spirits in colonial times. In seventeenth-century New Spain, for example, where the absolute control exercised by ecclesiastic doctrine in both church and lay matters did not freely tolerate such challenges, Sister Juana Inés de la Cruz dared to question social injustices. She conceived her mannered poetry in the best Spanish baroque tradition of the viceregal court and well within the confines of a neo-medieval church society. Nevertheless, in widely quoted quatrains,[2] she managed to condemn the double standard in the treatment of women and men, and in a lesser known "Christmas Carol Dedicated to Saint Peter Nolasco," she exposed the prejudicial attitude held by both white colonists and the church towards suffering black slaves. However, of all the works by this woman of genius, hailed as the Tenth Muse, one prose piece written within the rhetorical tradition of neo-Scholastic reasoning has preserved her voice for future generations as the first woman born in the Spanish New World who defended her own and her sisters' right to be educated. In *The Poetess's Rejoinder to the Very Illustrious Sister, Sor Filotea de la Cruz* (1691)—"Sor Filotea de la Cruz" being an alias for the Bishop of Puebla—she extolled pagan and Christian wise women in an autobiographic defense of her own quest for all types of knowledge, lay as well as religious, in the service of her church: "However, my lady, what can we women know other than kitchen philosophy? After all, Lupercio Leonardo said that one can well philosophize and yet cook a meal, to which I would add, when I see such things, that if Aristotle had been a cook, much more would he have written."[3]

So we see that at the threshold of the Age of Reason in the colony of New Spain, Sor Juana embodied both Old World traditions and New World spirit. Her critical concern for the social fabric of Old Mexico and her thirst for knowledge gleaned through experimentation and rational observation stood in direct opposition to the dictates of her church-dominated society, even for those with greater freedom of choice than a nun or a woman.

Whereas the colonies were culturally dominated by Spain and in the eighteenth and nineteenth centuries, before and after their independence, by France, today Spanish American authors such as those interviewed in this volume, have become more independent of European influences. Nevertheless, they are still attuned to the international cultural pulse, particularly if it is French. For example, Antonin Artaud's "theatre of cruelty" is reflected in the drama by the Argentinian Griselda Gambaro; the psychoanalytical theories of Jacques Lacan impress Luisa Valenzuela; and the "new novel" holds an attraction for the Cuban-born Julieta Campos. With the dawning of the Age of Modernity in Latin America, these persistent foreign influences were perceived by another Cuban, the visionary José Martí, as the legacy of Spanish America's cultural and economic dependence. He observed, "We were a masquerade in English trousers, Parisian vest, North American jacket and Spanish hat."[4] Martí called for greater cultural self-reliance and for the emergence of Spanish America from bondage by forging its own identity on autochthonous models.

Yet the coexistence or comingling of foreign or international styles with autochthonous themes continues to characterize contemporary Spanish American literature. For example, Julieta Campos's two novels, *Tiene los cabellos rojizos y se llama Sabina* (A Redhead Named

Sabina) and *El miedo de perder a Eurídice* (Fear of Losing Eurydice), while rich in allusions to a wide range of international cultural phenomena, also soulfully evoke her insular Caribbean origins and her adopted Mexican land. Marta Traba and Luisa Valenzuela often utilize internationally recognized narrative techniques in their novels, but the former also resuscitates the art of the colonial chronicler while the latter takes soundings of the native mythic substrata beneath contemporary Latin American events.

Although these authors may well conform to modern culture, in general "defined by its extraordinary freedom to ransack the world storehouse and to engorge any and every style it comes upon,"[5] such syncretism must be viewed in its Latin American context. It is an innate cultural trait that first surfaced in colonial times in accord with the demographic profile of each viceroyalty and capitania. There the characteristic propensity to meld the distinct customs of the Old and New Worlds first emerged with the coexistence of Catholic and indigenous rites and later with the intermingling of Christian and African religious rituals. When this syncretism spread to lay ceremonies, it prepared the way for the "engorging" of cultures that was to mark the Age of Modernity in Latin American literature.

One example of syncretism in lay ceremonies took place in New Spain in 1680 on the occasion of the arrival of the new viceroy. A good friend of Sor Juana Inés de la Cruz, the Creole astrologer and mathematician Carlos de Sigüenza y Góngora, was commissioned to execute the design of a traditional triumphal arch, which was customarily decorated with allegorical representations from classical Greek and Roman mythology. However, since Sigüenza y Góngora possessed a deep consciousness of the aboriginal heritage of his land and had assembled the most valuable collection in his time of archaeological and historical materials on the Aztec civilization, he chose to break abruptly with tradition by ignoring classical models for the triumphal arch and by adorning it, instead, with autochthonous representations of the feats of Aztec kings. In this way, he extolled the rich New World heritage scorned by the Spaniards[6] and superimposed it on the customary Old World arch.

Across the span of centuries from colonial times to the present, Sigüenza y Góngora's desire to praise and affirm that which is "American" led similarly inclined authors and artists to describe the diverse

22

facets of America's cities and countrysides, plains and mountain ranges, jungles and skyscrapers, pyramids and baroque cathedrals, emphasizing the heterogeneity of their heritage and the disparate pace of development of their culture. In the eyes of both Spanish and non-Spanish readers, telluric narratives for many years dominated Latin American literature, pitting civilization against barbarism in Manichean fashion and circumscribing its definition to regional and national themes and struggles.[7] Unfortunately, some commentators nowadays still judge Latin American fiction according to this literary style, as if in order to be "really" Latin American, literature must be populated by Indians or gauchos or must pit the civilized city against the untamed jungles and pampas. Perhaps this could be so if all of Latin America shared a common geography, demography, and development on economic, social, political, and aesthetic levels, and if its writers lived and practiced their profession within their national boundaries ignorant of the jet age and mass communication. However, this is obviously not the case.

In the first half of this century, the magnetism of Europe and of Paris, in particular, still prevailed for Latin American writers, who traveled widely and resided abroad. Consequently, many were nourished by a distanced perspective of their own lands. For example, the Guatemalan novelist, Miguel Angel Asturias, while working with Georges Raynaud on the Mayan *Popol-Vuh,* and the Cuban Alejo Carpentier, while exploring Leo Frobenious's and Pablo Picasso's interests in primitive cultures, both rediscovered the magical quality of their own New World cultures when they were far from their homelands. Later, many writers like Griselda Gambaro, Marta Traba, and Luisa Valenzuela would live for a time, or permanently, in exile, sometimes involuntary, in Europe and the United States and would perpetuate a similar pattern: viewing America from a distance during an epoch when Latin American literature would no longer be judged by its strict adherence to telluric reality. Instead, many writers would preserve their roots while reflecting the heterogenous and mutable modern culture to which they belong.

Many of these contemporary authors have come to sense a creative community that reaches well beyond national boundaries and even beyond the arts to the sciences and related areas of humanistic inquiry such as anthropology, psychology, and mythology. However, their interests often stand in opposition to logical scientific inquiry. Science seeks to codify and classify the relativistic phenomena of cultures and the mutable behavior of modern man, to order the universe into paradigmatic systems, to harness the historical fragments of chaos into a timeless, harmonious construct. Many Spanish American authors are less concerned with scientific absolutes and objectivity and more interested in recognizing the magical qualities that transform Latin American reality into a mythology (such as is apparent in the works of Elvira Orphée and Gabriel García Márquez) and in exploring the transcendental nature of archetypical initiations and regenerations of Latin Americans in search of their identity (examples of which are present in the works of Luisa Valenzuela and Julio Cortázar). These authors perceive change subsumed into a more eternal, repetitive scheme and are bent upon unearthing the hidden forces that shape their own continents.

In fact, the six authors in this volume share a poetic expression of reality described by the Mexican Octavio Paz as the original language of society, and in its passion and sensitivity, the language of all revelations and revolutions.[8] For it is with passion and sensitivity that authors such as Traba and Valenzuela capture and portray the America of social change and challenge (revolution), while others like Orphée evoke the timeless America of origins and roots (revelation). The nature of this lyrical approximation also varies, producing heterogenous styles. For example, Marta Traba's profession as an art critic influenced her expressionistic imagery and her ability to create atmospheres like that of the gray homogeneity in the impoverished urban ghetto. Perhaps the Mexican Juan Rulfo is her only equal in his lyrical approach to rural poverty. Armonía Somers's incomparable neo-baroque imagery and syntax envelop the reader as if trying to fill with words the existential void experienced by her characters in their solitude and despair. Luisa Valenzuela alters her environment by critical distancing through techniques of irony and parody; Elvira Orphée fathoms the raw passions of humankind, revealing cosmogonies as a "geographer and historian of heaven and hell."[9] And, finally, Griselda Gambaro distils pain and cruelty from the solitary lives of the "strange and the damned"[10] and projects them with black humor on a giant screen of grotesque proportions.

This poetic vision influences not only perspective and style but also narrative structures in the case of some. Julieta Campos's novels are often based on radial reading as in poetry where reiteration, polysemy, and antithesis impede a unilateral, fixed interpretation. Her novelistic structures, as well as some of Valenzuela's and Traba's, exemplify the fragmented polymorphic "open work"[11] with its characteristic ambiguity, multiple viewpoints, and analogical, rather than logical, concatenation of events. This type of open structure, along with some narrative collections by Orphée, Traba, and Valenzuela that cannot be classified definitely as either short stories or novels, blur the barriers between literary genres. This tendency toward ambiguous forms has evolved from the truncated, short "anti-novels" written in the 1920s and 1930s by Latin American vanguard writers such as Pablo Neruda, Vicente Huidobro, and Pablo Palacio. But they, too, inherited their centrifugal treatment of narrative structure from writers before the turn of the century during a period when innovation prevailed in literature and reflected the breakdown of traditional values in Latin American societies.

The rapid socioeconomic changes of the 1880s brought about by burgeoning industrialization and modernization, by the loss of tradition due to migrations to the cities, and by the widening horizons created by mass transport and media served to decentralize Latin American societies. Emphasis was placed on change and mobility, productivity and materialism. Artists began to mirror and criticize those societal upheavals. In 1882, Martí detailed the tumultuous, contradictory times, the absence of great works of outstanding and sustained majesty, and the confusion of minds preoccupied by thoughts that matured in the streets without time for meditation or organization.[12] In literature, tradition succumbed to modernization: genre forms were fractured, prose poems were cultivated, the fragmented novelistic structure appeared more frequently, and nonfiction insinuated itself into eclectic narratives until finally, in the twentieth century, the novel withdrew to its last refuge, language itself—as the Mexican Emilio Pacheco observed—to occupy territories that were once the domain of verse.[13]

Many astute critics of modern Latin American literature have noted this poetic phenomenon, which is particularly important for an understanding of the six authors in this study. Among those critics, the Uruguayan Angel Rama has alluded to the lyricism and intimate nature of Armonía Somers's fiction, characterizing it by a subjectivity that seems to shun the world while at the same time critically recognizing a more far-reaching sphere of reality on the level of an intense, personal experience. By extension, we might say that these six authors exemplify, in varying degrees, the type of orientation ascribed by Rama to Somers: their works relate intense, personal experiences, perhaps more representative of the authentic conditions of society than other so-called more realistic literature.[14] For much like their literary ancestors at the dawning of the Age of Modernity in Latin America, these women utilize their medium as a mirror to reflect society and a forum in which to criticize it; as a balm to salve wounds inflicted on them in their often alienated role as marginal commentators; and as an arena for deconstructing and reconstructing reality.

For some of them the creative process itself becomes the subject of their fiction as it had also been for some "modernista" writers in the late nineteenth century, vanguard writers in the earlier decades of this century, and their contemporaries like Julio Cortázar and Salvador Elizondo. For example, Luisa Valenzuela wages a linguistic battle against the paralysis of language in her semantic/somatic inquiries, thus continuing the century-old struggle against antiquated forms of expression and thought in Latin America; Julieta Campos questions her own contradictory attachment to the criticism of literary traditions and explores the process of writing as a novelistic theme. Thus in a self-reflexive mode, many of these authors fulfill one of the modern "oppositions"—against their own aesthetic expression—by desacralizing and demythologizing art as high culture by doing violence to it.

Violence abounds in many forms in the fiction of these six women. It is a violence, however, inherent in the literatures and cultures of their continents, as Ariel Dorfman has aptly perceived in *Imagination and Violence in America* in which he discusses only male authors.[15] It is a violation of language, the reader, humankind, and the comfortable, complacent, middle class way of life. For most of these women authors, violence is a visceral experience, a corporal agony/pleasure that heightens their awareness of their own beings and catapults them beyond themselves into mythic, existential, or primordial dimensions. Perhaps Clarice Lispector's character G. H. best portrays one aspect of that violence when her very being is altered by the cruel act of crushing a cockroach and then tasting its oozing milky, salty substance in a ritual that connects her with herself and with her primordial roots:

The serene woman that I had always been, had she gone mad with pleasure? With my eyes still closed I was quaking with exultation. To have killed: it was so much greater than I, it was as high as the boundless room that contained me. To have killed opened the aridity of the sands of the room to the damp, at last, at last, as if I had dug and dug with hard and eager fingers until I discovered within myself the drinkable thread of life which, in reality, was the thread of death. I slowly opened my eyes, gently now, in gratitude and diffidence, ashamed of my splendor. . . . How else could I describe that horrible, cruel thing that was there—raw material and dry plasma—as I retreated within myself with dry nausea, I slipping centuries and centuries into the slime. It was slime and not even slime long since desiccated but slime still moist and alive. It was a slime in which the roots of my identity writhed with unbearable sluggishness.[16]

Whether using details of the intense personal experience that Rama referred to and that Lispector exemplifies so well, or employing the lyrical language of revelation and rebellion that Paz alluded to, the six women writers of this volume spin their yarn from the fiber of their souls and their national consciousness. Although their texts emerge from multiple and diverse contexts, they are modern searches that question and criticize without necessarily providing solutions to dilemmas. As Valenzuela affirms, "All personal searches respond to numerous exigencies that many share. There is no individual who develops outside of her society. . . . We are all answering or posing new questions that are the heritage of every human being."[17]

Armonía Somers

Uruguay

I behold the fury of visceral impulses.

Clarice Lispector

Armonía Somers.

Given name, Armonía Etchepare de Henestrosa. Born in Uruguay, 1920. Married Rodolfo Henestrosa. Taught in Montevideo. Delegate from Library and Museum of Education for bibliographic selection to Inter-American Seminar on Elementary Education at Organization of American States and UNESCO, 1950. Received prize from Ministry of Public Education and Social Planning of Uruguay for *El derrumbamiento,* 1953. Assistant director of National Library and Museum of Education; received prizes from Municipality of Montevideo and University of the Republic for *Educación de la adolescencia,* 1957. Member of Commission for Certification of Teachers, Montevideo, 1958. Invited by United Nations to work on crime prevention and the treatment of delinquents in London; member of Commission on Texts for the National Council of Elementary Education and Teacher Training, 1960. Director of National Museum of Education; editor of *Boletín Informativo de la Biblioteca y Museo Pedagógicos;* founder and editor of journal of Center for Educational Documentation and Dissemination, *Documentum,* 1961. Representative from Montevideo to Seminar on Education for Development and Social Progress at United Nations, 1962. Director of National Center for Educational Documentation and Dissemination, 1962–71. Received internship from UNESCO to study education in Paris, Dijon, Geneva, and Madrid, 1964. Attended First Latin American Conference of Directors of Centers for Educational Documentation and Information in Argentina, 1966. Editor of *Anales* and *Enciclopedia de Educación,* 1967–71. Member of Commission on Texts for the National Council of Elementary Education and Teacher Training, 1968. Received prizes from Uruguayan Ministry of Education and Culture and from City of Montevideo for *Un retrato para Dickens,* 1969. Delegate from National Council of Elementary Education and Teacher Training to UNESCO Commission on the International Year of the Book, 1971. Abandoned her career in education to dedicate herself to writing fiction, 1972.

31

"Everything is uncanny, strange, disconcerting, repulsive and, at once incredibly fascinating in the most unusual prose that the history of our literature has known: Armonía Somers's books."[1] Thus, Angel Rama dispensed with all other Uruguayan antecedents in his evaluation of Somers in 1963. Nevertheless, three years later in his description of the "strange and the damned" writers of Uruguayan literature, he suggested a spiritual kinship between Somers's fiction and that of the French-Uruguayan Isidore Ducasse, the count of Lautréamont.[2] In fact, both Somers and Lautréamont do share certain propensities: both focus on the cruel and solitary nature of man, who is quite as bestial as any animal; on eroticism and sexual violations; on desacralizing God; on a repugnant and visceral depiction of humanity; and on descriptions of nightmarish atmospheres. Somers, like Lautréamont before her, challenges the hypocrisy of social and religious morality and rebels against solitude, fate, and death devoid of the promise of paradise.

The women, men, and children in her novels and short stories are often assassins, rapists, madmen, vagabonds, prostitutes, lesbians, drunkards, orphans, or malcontents. Others are barely living, relating their last moments of life. This world and the beyond fuse in a narrative in which the living and the dead often share a common sense of emptiness and a lack of communication. The young man in the short novel *De miedo en miedo* (From One Fear to the Next), for example, finds a female companion—"We are like two bodies inside the same skin"—and then loses her: "And I had just realized it because one of the two wanted to abandon it, to recover her own form."[3] Somers seems to sympathize with these antiheroes for her irreverent irony is often balanced with tenderness, especially towards some of the characters who are based on acquaintances of hers: "Perhaps because I have such a need for pieces of flesh to exorcise myself, I am understanding where my characters are concerned."[4]

For Somers, creativity is never an enjoyable game but rather always painful; it is a disemboweling, a dismemberment. The young man in *De miedo en miedo* expresses her feelings: "Then I decided to buckle under to custom like any old man riding a bus, tight-lipped though his thoughts keep tugging away like a dog who found a tree, held back by his master, yet free to pee on the conventions of a morality chock full of rules, of a language prickling with barbs that martyr the mind of those who have to write or speak for the rest of the slaves."[5]

This passage exemplifies one of the accomplishments of Somers's prose style: her expressionistic flair, based on the unconventional juxtaposition of visceral and at times repulsive or violent imagery and a lyrical reflection on life.

In her descriptions, the body—hair, tongue, innards—often undergoes bizarre transformations that render it an ephemeral object. The most insignificant details attain existential importance: "And to give the woman all of the hairs so that every morning she can take stock of how many she has gathered to later form with the pile, the pillow of her life."[6] Corporal solidity is denied when twin boys climb to a roof where "the wind high above puffed them up like pieces of clothing on a line," or when a dead body is found "converted into a gray rag and suddenly deflated like a parachute caught in the brambles."[7] The body disintegrates like "a piece of porcelain that has been broken while over the pieces we keep watch with accustomed care."[8] In this sensorial imagery, the body's humors—sweat, saliva, milk, blood, semen—evoke the most basic physical nature of human relationships: "The woman had become completely liquid. She was a viscous and salty mixture of tepid tears, mucous, anguish, semen. And so, entirely dissolved, she flowed into his blood like a virus for the rest of that unexpected shipwreck in which they both felt themselves lost even before they began."[9]

Ever since *La mujer desnuda* (The Naked Woman) was published, Somers has continued to address the topics of sexuality and eroticism. That first allegorical novel scandalized provincial Montevideo of the 1950s, whose critics condemned her as a "gifted and pathological erotic," a "misguided pedagogue," and a "cryptomaniac recidivist."[10] Somers explored the sexual aggression of misogynists in short stories like "El despojo" (Plunder) and female eroticism in passages like the following from "El hombre del túnel" (The Man in the Tunnel):

> Suddenly, while the elevator door opened automatically like a
> well-lubricated vagina, the greasy stairway bannister winked at
> me again with the guile of a faun from behind the trees. The
> exact amount of time for the door to close again. And there I
> was losing myself, astride the bannister, just as someone must
> have invented them for incipient orgasms that later on over-
> power the ripe sex in bloom until it ends up contracting like a
> burnt rag in old age.[11]

Only in rare cases are sexual relationships portrayed as tender and
beautiful, for in Somers's prose indifference and pernicious eroticism
predominate. Nevertheless, she deals unabashedly and lyrically with
issues still considered taboo in her society: a lesbian relationship is
sympathetically recorded by the curious son of one of the women; a
peasant's breasts swell with milk from the desire to have a child as a
stranger suckles at her nipple; and in "Salomón" (Solomon), a virile
woman bartender gives a baby away to a prostitute, deciding in favor
of the woman who truly cares for him, instead of his mother. Both the
female Solomon and the lesbian mother symbolize stereotypes of
"businesswomen" whose roles are on the fringes of what society per-
mits in Spanish America.

But Somers's sensitivity to female/male relationships creates even
more unique and interesting interchanges with regard to the sensations
of sexuality. When the peasant woman allows herself to be suckled by
the stranger, the narrator describes the man's thoughts in a way that
recalls his earlier rape of a young girl; the milk, like the semen before,
enters the body rendering the recipient—before the raped girl, now the
rapist—a helpless victim: "And so without a chance to even rub away
the light of day, they tell you you're a little boy, they make you cuddle
up in the haystack, they rock you to sleep, they shove you who knows
where, they invade you, they penetrate you."[12] In *De miedo en miedo,*
the male protagonist experiences birth, the birth of fear: "The night I
gave birth, I was a man."[13]

Perhaps the most unusual treatment, at least within the Spanish
American context, of stereotypes, both sexual and racial, occurs in the
short story "El derrumbamiento" (The Cave-In). Two major cultural
constants—"machismo" and the cult of the Virgin Mary, "maria-
nismo"—come into play when a black man fleeing from the police
seeks refuge in a shack for transients in which the patron saint and
protector is a statue of the Virgin Mary. In his delirious state, the

black man imagines the Virgin Mary leaving her pedestal and kneeling before him to implore him to free her from immobility so that she can avenge her son's death. In order to gain liberty, she commands the feverish man, Tristán, to massage her entire body to melt the wax from her flesh. The black man fights his sacrilegious desire for the holy Virgin, who urges him on but finally denies him by claiming that man's true glory lies in knowing how to seduce a virgin rather than having intercourse with her.

The two protagonists are rendered as antithetical symbols of traditional good and evil for the black man is tender while the Virgin is seductively aggressive and critical of the esteem in which humanity has held her: "Since they made me out of marble, of wax, of carved wood, of gold, of ivory, of lies, I no longer possess that grief. And I have to live like that, lying with this stupid smile they've put on my face. Tristán, I wasn't what they've painted me to be. I was different, and certainly less beautiful. And it is for what I am going to tell you that I have descended."[14] She is the manifestation of two major biblical roles conferred by Spanish American Catholic societies on women: that of the seductress Eve and that of the virgin mother of God, Mary. She depends on a man to release her from the bondage contrived by men, and yet she saves the black man from the police at the end of the story, for as she escapes through the window, she brings down the shack in a cave-in that kills them all, including Tristán.

Somers frequently deals with death in her fiction. In one of her most accomplished short stories, "El entierro" (The Burial), pathetic and macabre descriptions alternate with a keen sense of black humor in a tale about the adventures of a bunch of drunkards who lose their friend's corpse on the way to the cemetery. During our interview, Somers explained her fascination with and fear of death: "I always have that condiment of death in my creative kitchen because in so doing I wish to dominate death so it will not do so to me."

During the interview, the author sat in an armchair, with an "occupied" sign pinned to it, in a sixteenth-floor apartment where the window boxes that should store awnings are filled instead with bats. Somers refuses to scare them off because she feels them to be part of high-rise living in the "Salvo Palace" apartment building where she lives. Offhandedly she alluded to her interest in the Kabbala and occult botany, her passion for biscuits, her distractions when she writes near the window where doves peck lovingly at each other, and her faith in a language of the trees. At that time it seemed to me that from those surroundings, Somers had extracted the beauty and ugliness of nature and man. Like some literary alchemist she had filtered them into a crucible where words transformed the base metals of existence into the precious metaphor of man's loneliness and abandonment: "There are things that cannot be said, not because of what they express but because of the solitude they encompass. A plundered orange grove can speak, a man who's lost his liver, a medal whose engraving has been rubbed away. But a solitary cry will fill the air—unheard, a shriek of trees bared of oranges, a man without his liver, a medal worn down by time."[15]

———

Montevideo, Uruguay   *14–15 July 1978*

How did you begin to write fiction?

La mujer desnuda was my first novel; it emerged from within like a kind of lava that lay dormant in me due to fear or bias or because I was involved in other pursuits. *La mujer desnuda* was born in a dream. One night I dreamt that I severed my head from my body and placed it on a tray, and then like Salomé, I walked around the room holding it, but without losing the ability to think. My head continued to function until, all of a sudden, I put it back on and realized that I was no longer going to be the same for that decapitation had left me with a new sense of independence. And so that woman whose head had been recovered could not be like other women. Then the novel began to write itself. When that woman replaced her head as if it were a war helmet, she altered her actions. Her past doesn't appear in the novel, but one can conjecture: a woman wrenched from a stem like a flower to live free. Perhaps she was married, had children, birthdays (conventional ones). So she leaves the shack, naked as she was in the dream, to wander through the countryside. Everything she does from then on is licit; she shockingly attacks the prejudices of a world based on absurdities. As I wrote that novel, I felt very liberated even though the first draft had many structural defects because I wrote it in about a month and a half. I showed it to some friends who directed a magazine; they decided to publish it. But it wasn't until I began to write short stories, later on, that I realized how much more leeway fiction offered me in comparison to nonfiction for I could play with that reality in a game that freed me. And so "El derrumbamiento" was born, a short story based on a true life situation. They told me about that house, which was about to cave in, where delinquents sought refuge from the police. They said a candle burned before a statue of the Virgin in a corner of that shack. Then came the creative part, a mixture of reality and fiction to which I became addicted, sort of like a drug addict but in a different sense because I was comfortable with it and could do as I pleased.

So you never tried to write fiction as a child or adolescent?

Oh, no. Never. I began with the novel. Once in Chile, they asked me how it was that I had been born so mature. I didn't know how to answer because during my childhood and adolescence I was very busy with my studies, very responsible; I had to graduate, begin my career. I must have had a bad reputation among my fellow students. I had no time then to write, except what was required of me as a student.

Did you enjoy reading fiction when you were a child?

No, I didn't read fiction. I suppose I read all of Jules Verne, who invented what he wrote. He never moved from his desk, but read books about travel and geography and so based his fiction on reality. Jules Verne was a favorite of mine and *Les Misérables* by Victor Hugo.

The classics.

Yes. I didn't read pure invention.

Do you consider yourself part of a specific literary generation in Uruguay?

No, I feel no ties with the generation I ought to be part of. I believe that apart from the usual generations, the literary ones are not only chronological but also imply a certain homogeneity of form, motivation, semantics, and even in ideology, that separates them from previous or future generations. In my case (not because I feel superior or inferior, but rather different), I do not consider myself to be part of the generation that they usually call mine.

Are there any specific literary influences in your work?

There has been a lot of discussion about that. Fortunately, it has ceased; in fact, so many influences had been attributed to me that I felt like the "daughter of influences." At first the critics couldn't understand how something original could occur to me. Now it seems that I *am* original, but in those days, I wasn't. One person, who will remain nameless, even said that I was the product of reader indigestion. I've never told anyone about the few writers who have had an impact on me, and nobody has discovered them. So I enjoy myself a lot when critics name Maupassant or some Russian for it just so happens that I was dazzled by Proust and his novelistic skill, his loving care for detail. I thought to myself, what a craftsman; he abandons the novel as he describes, but at the same time he is creating marvels. He taught us all when he held our hands and urged us to linger over details. When I reread my works, I realize I do not write at all like Proust, but that doesn't mean he was not my teacher. And I confess it because many share him with me, but don't say so. And there's another author who has had an impact on my work, Strindberg. His cynical view made me look at things differently than I had before.

In a critical way?

Yes, the fiercely critical manner in which Strindberg saw marriage, as if two beings were united by the arteries of their sexual organs.

In what way has your fiction been influenced by your profession as a teacher and librarian?

Not at all. They are separate pursuits because they embody two personalities. I can feel where they part company. As a writer, I was never a teacher, but as a teacher I was a writer, and so my classes were very imaginative and stimulating. The children were hypnotized when I taught a lesson, so much so that when I fell ill or asked for a leave and a substitute came to replace me, they misbehaved, jumping through windows, doing all kinds of things. So, one day when I heard that, I asked them, "What ever came over you? You're such charming children," and one answered, "We were bored." But as a writer I was never didactic because that would have been frightful. I write that way in my other profession, in pedagogical essays, not in the novel.

As you've explained, you began writing novels. How do you perceive the difference between the novel and the short story as genres? How do you decide which one you are about to write?

I feel very comfortable with the short story. They say that genre is more difficult because it requires synthesis; one has to present a macrocosm within a microcosmic plot which may transpire over several years. For example, in "El desvío" [Off course] a couple lives together for years that are compressed into a train trip suggestive of the passage of time, of growing old. I feel very much at ease with that synthesis. Now, I consider the novel a more amenable genre than the short story because the novel is a daily exercise; it's sitting down to caress the theme, the characters, to play with them and lead them along so they can't get lost. That makes me feel happy. But when I'm about to write a short story, I know it's to be a short story, and the same with the novel. Perhaps it's intuition. For example, with *Sólo los elefantes encuentran mandrágora* [Only Elephants Find Mandrake Roots], I knew it was a novel because from the start I imagined it as a novel. I thought that if I had squeezed it into a short story it would be like putting two liters of water into a one-liter bottle.

It seems to me that in the first novel you describe Rebecca Linke's nakedness, her liberty at the age of thirty, in terms of her encounter with love and death which serves as a catalyst in awakening hidden desires in the people of a town bound by moral and religious slavery. Is there an allegorical intention implied?

Yes, possibly. If the intent wasn't there, the allegory was, because at times one doesn't mean to do something but it happens anyway. I truly feel that breaking the chains that bind one and risking one's life is not only Rebecca Linke's drama, we all share in it. It is a holocaust.

How was La mujer desnuda *received by the public and the critics?*

They were divided. In general the novel made its way into the hands of the intellectuals because they were the ones who bought *Clima*, a magazine dedicated to the arts. The general public didn't read it. The intellectuals formed two groups, those who repudiated the novel (I never knew why, perhaps because they sensed themselves to be identified with some character) and those who felt hypnotized by the novel. I had the privilege of attending a round table discussion on *La mujer desnuda* in the home of a painter. I went, not as the author, but as "Woman X," even though the painter knew it was my book. I remember how cold it was that night as we sat around the wood stove, and finally we ran out of logs. The discussion continued as they tore me to shreds, and the painter began to burn picture frames to keep the studio warm. One man, who was the most vicious slanderer of them all (afterwards I realized that he had seen himself reflected in one of the characters), referring to the woodsman whose wife is old and passionless, said, "How can a man be so cruel as to abuse the woman after having worked and fought at her side?" Then I, who was not Armonía Somers, but rather Woman X, said, "Maybe because the woodsman was dead, the way you are, until the naked woman aroused him; and no one knows what can happen when one is awakened." That brief but suggestive answer (where could I have learned that?) was, perhaps, one of the ways in which, later, I was discovered to be the author. But as for the public, there was no opportunity to read that first novel. When Tauro Publishers brought out an edition in 1967, I had already established myself in literary circles and was no longer criticized cruelly. Later on the critics produced fine studies, and I was respected. The novel could be read without risk. Times have changed, I suppose; between 1950 and 1967, the public evolved. The book became available to the young who are sharper judges, freer of preconceptions, cleaner. So they see purity where there is none; whereas, an old, mature man transmits his own filth to what he reads. Such was the case, for example, with the short story "El derrumbamiento." One man who heard about it bought the book and brought it home to his wife. Afterwards, he himself read the story and nearly died. "How is it that I bought my wife that book with such a terrible, dirty plot about an impending sexual relationship between the Virgin Mary and a black man?" Well, I really got furious then. And so one day when I ran into him, I said, "Tell me, don't you have a picture of the Immaculate Virgin in your bedroom? And isn't she watching what you do in bed?"

The Virgin Mary is only one of many biblical references in your fiction. In La mujer desnuda *and* Un retrato para Dickens *(A Portrait for Dickens), the bible seems to serve as a structural base for the stories.*

I consider the bible to be the greatest novel ever written, a serialized novel. In it there is poetry, drama, inconceivable massacres that today we call terrorism; we've forgotten that terrorism is nothing new. The fact that in *Un retrato para Dickens* I took the part about Tobias from the bible is due to the novel's setting in a tenement building where a parrot was kept on the patio. I wanted to use that parrot as a kind of narrator who saw the action from above (a sort of bird's-eye view), whereas the little girl saw it from a human perspective. But the parrot perceived the action as the reincarnation of an ancient experience. And Asmodeo came to mind, the Asmodeo in the biblical pages about

Tobias. To me the parrot represented the devil, Asmodeo. You see in me there is a kind of religiosity I try to transform into irreverence, so much so that in my latest novel, *Sólo los elefantes encuentran mandrágora,* I call God an atheist. I figure that God is the only one who cannot believe in himself, and that is why he believes in others. He exists, but he cannot say, "I believe in God." Possibly I have this conflict because I am the daughter of a die-hard anticlerical father. In this novel he appears as a very strange character. My father may have had the same conflict.

Why did you entitle your second novel Un retrato para Dickens?

When I saw a photograph of my friend as a child, I associated it with my idea of Oliver Twist. I saw the photograph after I had already conceived the thread of the novel. That friend of mine made some comments about her life, the first ten years of her life, a sort of synthesis of everything—rape, the beginning of adolescence, relationships with adults, and the tenement with the parrot. I stored all of that information away until one day she produced the photograph that set it all loose. If I hadn't seen the picture, perhaps there'd be no novel.

You divided the novel into three points of view: the young girl's, the parrot Asmodeo's, and a biblical third voice.

That's a characteristic of mine that may have to do with my activities as a documentalist. There is a tendency in me to systematize, and I am grateful for it because it forces me to see things clearly. Documentation organizes knowledge and in a novel if one didn't order ideas, they could pour forth like champagne from a bottle. Then there would be no novel, just a wasted gush.

Speaking of champagne. I didn't understand why you included recipes for biscuits in the novel.

Of course, the little girl has an obsession with biscuits. The word melted in her mouth, but she didn't know how they tasted because she was so poor that she could barely eat a piece of bread. And so I created a cult to biscuits. The cookbook exists. It's an old book of fifty-seven recipes. But all this is not just gab between two women who have nothing more to do except exchange recipes during a telephone conversation. It is a real anguish that the girl feels, she yearns to taste biscuits. And I'm going to confess something to you. That was my anguish. As a child I always wanted to eat biscuits but had nothing more than bread. I used to visit with some Basque women who had a dairy and took in ironing, and when I smelled a marvelous aroma issuing forth from the kitchen, they would say to me, "You smell biscuits." So the smell of biscuits became a sort of paradise for me, and I contented myself with that fragrance from heaven.

If I remember correctly, in that novel, the black boy avenges the young girl's rape (he considers her his sister) by killing the idiot who attacked her. And in the story "El derrumbamiento," a black man is seduced by the Virgin Mary. Can you explain your interest in literary characters who are black?

In the case of the Virgin, I had to make her come alive at the hands of the humblest of all men, for she, too, had suffered, according to the myth. It had to be a man pursued by the law and, implicitly, persecuted due to his color. I respect the black race (and that has nothing at all to do with the book *Roots*); I sympathize with all those who suffer from impotence in the face of injustice.

In the story there is an erotic scene. And in your fiction in general, the erotic episodes and descriptions are usually violent. You speak of loving someone by destroying him; there are rapes, hatred between men and women, abortions, misogyny, and sexual desire that borders on death.

Well, eroticism is a reality. I don't mean to say that I treat it with contempt but rather naturally. However, destruction is something else again. One destroys in order to swallow up another person; love is ravaging the other in order to incorporate him into one self. We don't devour the male the way the female spider does after copulating; but in both men and women a destructive element is present in love, destruction in order to take possession. It must be an idea Freud explained. The eroticism that appears in my fiction is not mine, it's what I see in the world, and only hypocrites would deny that.

But it seems to me that in your fiction, the woman is almost always the victim in such encounters, with the exception, perhaps, of the women in the third section of "El despojo," or in the story "Requiem por Goyo

Rivera" (Requiem for Goyo Rivera), the two women who are childless, one has an abortion and the other is sterile.

As a sort of punishment.

Both seem to be seeking revenge against their men by not giving them children.

Yes. You must have noticed that I tend to create paradigms. Those two women unfortunately exist.

Still, in your fiction, it seems that erotic violence is usually perpetrated by men on women.

No. I don't see it that way. No. There is always a superbly refined and mysterious vengeance in women. In *La mujer desnuda* I named one woman Antonia. I was seeking revenge because the naked woman says, "I don't want any names that can be changed to a man's name by altering just one letter." I was sending a message to someone; it was my revenge.

There are quite a few lesbian characters in your works.

I try to deal with lesbianism poetically; I don't consider it to be as terrible as male homosexuality. Aesthetically it's different. Homosexuality in ancient Greece was poetic because the Greeks dealt with the body in a special way. But the case of two ugly men can be repulsive. The contact between two hairy bodies must be horrible. Besides, in male homosexuality, a man, at times, humiliates himself and even risks his life for some worthless sort devoid of all refinement. But in the case of women, on the other hand, it seems there is a defense of the sex; they are defending themselves against men. In masculine homosexuality there is no such defense against women.

The only brotherhood or disinterested love between characters in your fiction occurs when two accomplices gang up on a third person. Moreover, there is no possibility of love between a man and a woman, unless it ends in death.

From the biblical perspective, mine is the Old Testament, an eye for an eye. Turning the other cheek like Christ isn't my cup of tea. So the spirit of reprisal that you've noticed is perhaps autobiographical. I do not pardon, I do not know how to forgive. Now your other idea that a perfect relationship between man and woman never comes about without a fatal ending, in general I would say that is so, unfortunately. Not that I believe that all love meets its mortal fate, but there is almost a sort of curse on great lovers, who always die. Romeo and Juliet.

Sometimes in your work, the traditional roles attributed to men and women deviate to produce short stories like "Salomón" in which the biblical judge is a female bartender or in De miedo en miedo *in which the male protagonist experiences the sensations of giving birth.*

Life is that way. A prostitute can be more tenderly maternal than the real mother of a child, and so the judge gives the baby to the former. A man can give birth to fear.

That kind of concretion of an obsession, anguish, or pain in order to exorcise it is a unique feature of your prose style.

Yes. Perhaps because I need to extract pieces from myself. I'm afraid of psychiatrists and have no respect for them. So I have a sympathetic attitude towards my characters, I'm the psychiatrist and I make them give birth to relieve themselves.

In the story "El entierro," you have achieved a fine sense of the macabre, of black humor. How did you come to write about that burial?

It's based on reality. The corpse was really lost during the funeral procession and floated downstream. Some elements are true and others exaggerated. Besides, I really understand the friendship men feel for one another, like in the story. Women experience that camaraderie less frequently. Those men went to the hospital to fetch their buddy Honoribaldo and then to get drunk with him, to celebrate his release from the hospital. That is something one would usually not see among women. We women have a word, "comadrear," to gossip, to talk, to do each other a little favor, to exchange recipes; but the intimacy of love, of friendship between men is extraordinary. That story is based on an episode in which a man transported a corpse to the cemetery by seating it by his side. If he hit a pothole in the road, he'd say, "Stay still, you, don't act that crazy." When someone told me that I found it amusing. And one day while reading the obituaries in the newspaper, I saw the name Honoribaldo Piedra. I know I said to myself, "What a lovely name for a character." But since I thought it might show a lack of respect, I changed the last name to Selva. Everything else was that downpour, that creative cascade that is unleashed around small anecdotes. The final macabre scene was pure invention.

One of your protagonists says that "thinking about death has always been your executioner." Would you explain your fascination with death?

Perhaps it is as one critic stated, a fascination with horror; maybe it's the fear I have of death, not my own because suicide has always attracted me. It must be uncanny to be able to unleash oneself and slip away. But I'm terrified by the death of others; so death is like a condiment. As the Arabs use cumin, so I always have that condiment of death in my creative kitchen because in so doing I wish to dominate death so it will not do so to me.

And the dead who seem more alive in your stories than the living?

Of course, that's the way it is. We bump elbows everyday with the living and end up considering them of little importance. But a dead man commands our attention. He stays with us, he stops when we do, goes to bed when we do, especially if he was a loved one, and so one feels how the dead are more alive than those who live.

There are certain symbols which are reiterated like leitmotifs in your prose: the circle, trees and rain, and the number seven. For example, whenever you refer to death or paradise, you mention that grass grows there and animals who look like men on all fours graze there; but there are no trees or rain.

Well, to use the words of the famous Uruguayan poet, Juana de Ibarbourou, I have a "wild root" that I've never divulged to anyone. Rain and trees speak to me in a special language, and I can converse with them. I see rain as a benediction, as a metaphysical shower as if the earth were thirsty and the rain knew of it. So I believed, even in my youth.

And what of the number seven in "El ángel planeador" (The Angel Who Landed), "El desvío," and "El hombre del túnel" (The Man at the End of the Tunnel)?

Wait one moment. I'd like to first clarify something. You know, I am an advocate of occult botany. That explains my interest in the mandrake. I consider plants to be mysterious beings that speak in metalanguage. And as for the number seven, it always arises because I'm also a Kabbalist; numbers come to me, and I add them up. They almost always total thirteen and seven. The number seven pursues me; I was born October seventh.

At this time, I wonder if we might turn to your own preference in Latin American fiction. Which contemporary writers do you read?
To be sincere I wouldn't like to give names or establish priorities. The "boom" of Latin American literature was a phenomenon of latent vitality, like a seed, similar to the energy conserved in the grains of wheat found in the pharaoh's tombs, grains which germinated thousands of years later. I am unaware of the catalyst which produced the collective eclosion in Latin America of the "boom." But the reason for my hesitancy concerning preferences has to do with historical proximity and thus a lack of perspective which would allow for an objective, dispassionate, and lasting scale of values.

Are there any women writers today who impress you?
Yes. The Chilean María Luisa Bombal. *La amortajada* [The Shrouded Woman] fascinated me. You know, I reread it in the summer during four months we spent in Somersville. While I am writing, I usually don't read much because I'm afraid of being influenced. Twenty-five years later, I discovered its symbolism. The half-opened eyes of the shrouded woman do not represent feminine literature (I have always maintained that sex is nonexistent in this realm), but rather woman's hermetic condition, her confrontation with truth after a living death during a lifetime. I hope that the rereading of other great women will allow me to clarify my opinion of them.

Do you feel there is such a phenomenon as "female writing"?
No, definitely not. There can be writing for women, a certain kind of easy reading; but literature has no sex. I don't share the idea of feminine literature, so when they say my books are masculine, I say they're literature, that's all.

Why do they characterize your work as masculine?
Because they say it has certain strength, a virility, a valor that a woman usually doesn't express due to ancestral prejudices which are of no

consequence to me. I believe it's good for women to gather, for women writers to assemble at conferences if they're going to discuss literature and not other problems. Besides, that spreads the news about our literature, which we ought to do since men are more prominent.

Would you like to tell me a little about the novel you are writing now, Sólo los elefantes encuentran mandrágora?

I hadn't written anything from 1969 to 1973; I simply couldn't. I went to see a doctor, not a psychiatrist, a general practitioner. He said that it would pass, and I shouldn't worry. Then one day I read the jacket of a Rachmaninoff record. And I discovered that the same thing had happened to him until, all of a sudden, as when a cap pops from pressure, the music came to him. The Somersville house had an attic, and one day I felt something strange inside, so I went upstairs and began to write and write and write for a year and a half. Of course, that first version of *Sólo los elefantes encuentran mandrágora* wasn't suitable in some respects, but it was a catharsis after a long silence. I admire self-discipline in a writer. I have very little.

By the way, when you write, do you need to work in a specific atmosphere?

No. I write anywhere. In an office, in noisy cafés, leaning on walls. But I become distracted a lot here, writing near the window that looks out on the trains and the doves that perch on the sill to bill and coo.

Does the situation of the female author in Spanish America differ from that of the male author? Does she have the same opportunities to publish her work and circulate it in her own country? Abroad? In translations? The same opportunities to win national or international literary prizes?

In Uruguay there is not a great deal of difference between the situations of a male or female author, aside from differing feminine or masculine sensitivities one might detect in the work itself. Due to great future-oriented national figures—both male and female—civil and political rights, education and employment opportunities, etc., are the same for everyone. In certain legal areas, on the contrary, a woman enjoys more rights than a man, as is the case when she requests a divorce from him without having to state the grounds and without his having the right to protest. As a result, writing, publishing, criticizing, defending, and the winning of national prizes are not activities or aspirations proscribed by competition or by exclusive masculine control. Perhaps only a vague aftertaste of ancestral prejudices relative to her own female condition can stop a woman writer, but almost never obstacles imposed by men. With few exceptions, when men break the rules for extraliterary motives, they take care to avoid sex discrimination as public judges of feminine creativity. On the contrary, with reference to editions, translations, and international prizes, marked differences are apparent. Man knows how to spread his nets on foreign waters so as to penetrate the market using all sorts of political resources, and even surreptitious self-aggrandizement. Many times, he even speculates with an air of persecuted ideologue, sometimes with reason, other times motivated only by the search for fertile lands. In tactics the woman author seems to lag behind while exercising an interior sensitivity to the vanguard on a clearly dignified level. We women will take a long time to adopt the Machiavellian motto as a way of life in literature. That is how we've been relegated to our present lack of status abroad.

Are there certain taboo themes for women writers that would be accepted more easily by society if the author were a man?

In the matter of themes that are taboo to women I can speak only with reference to my own work. My themes, my narrative contexts, my protagonists, and the underlying philosophy in all of my fiction could be indicted, but they were never forbidden me either explicitly or implicitly. I believe, rather, that passivity as a major malady belongs to both sexes and that literature is slowly liberating itself from that merely by evolving, especially when self-criticism is carried out systematically. For, if on the one hand, according to Starobinski, "literature as such does not belong exclusively to the world of reason," on the other hand, in the writer's laboratory delicate maturing processes occur which, without obliging us to age like parchment, impose on us a self-censure that is the most valid of all.

In your fiction, do you consciously or subconsciously broach themes that specifically pertain to the Spanish American woman? Are you concerned with woman's socioeconomic role in Spanish America?

My fictitious female characters have been universal up to now. Nevertheless, I'm not excluding the possibility of future creations with a specific view towards some continental feminine creature that could be paradigmatic in socioeconomic as well as in other realms. Themes and characters assault the writer without a great deal of premeditation on her part.

Recently, have you been able to earn a living exclusively by writing fiction?

No, it has never been possible for me to earn a living as an author of fiction, and this question and its answer call to mind so many dispossessed fellow artists that I feel as if I am in the midst of a great picturesque, dramatic family. Given the meager royalties which authors still earn, the anachronistic 10 percent which no one has succeeded in destroying like Poe's house of Usher in the swamp, and the half-literate masses who constitute a marginal economic class, I believe that exceptions occur with certain kinds of mass-produced best-sellers or by means of succulent prizes that change the writer's luck overnight.

What are you writing now? Does it sustain your interests expressed in earlier works? Are there new experiments, directions?

To a certain degree my last novel, *Sólo los elefantes encuentran mandrágora,* was an experiment to remedy what I had written before. But it will be your task, the critics', to decide whether a narrator finally has unmasked herself or whether she continues barricaded behind her fiction.

Presently, what kind of readings interest you most?

Right now I favor reading essays without distinguishing fields. But I always refer to works that seduce us by making us perceive how other winds are blowing today, how different data function to redefine or clarify the obscure, albeit in certain essays an apocalyptic vision may prevail.

There are many Spanish American writers who do not live or have not lived at some time in their own countries but rather have written from abroad—for political, social, or personal reasons—in voluntary or in-

voluntary exile: Cortázar, García Márquez, Vargas Llosa, Puig, Donoso. Does this situation apply to women writers from Spanish America? Do they feel the need or desire to distance themselves from their social context? Can they do so as easily as male authors?

Always from the point of view of the woman who concerns me, the Uruguayan-Hispano American, I must say that within the framework of her free will to choose an ideology or better yet a political conduct that takes her into exile or to distance herself in search of new possibilities, she walks with man in the contemporary diaspora. And, no doubt, she probably shares identical feelings of solitude, rootlessness, and the necessity to assimilate herself into countries which receive and protect her without loving her. But, also, it is certain that from Genesis to our day, Eve, the serpent, and the apple have comprised the best contrived legend within the larger spectrum of symbols.

Since we met for the interview, have you written other books? Would you describe the importance you attach to your recently published fiction?

In *Sólo los elefantes encuentran mandrágora,* and with total creative freedom, I tried to mix elements which are usually utilized by themselves to give a unified character to a certain kind of work: the universal with the regional; the intimate and psychological with the social; the political and their opposites; the scholarly with the empirical; the historical with the fictitious; the passage from country to city. Also, genres communicate with each other: the vulgar serialized story and the romantic atmosphere, occult hermeticism and popular superstitions, pure naturalism and magical realism, etc. By means of a division into chromatic periods with a certain somewhat chaotic alteration of the time—since the protagonist herself is a version of "hell"—I think I've achieved that type of experiential pouring forth and inventiveness that leave authors ready for hibernation, that is, a more or less prolonged period of lethargy until some propitious spring awakens them again.

Griselda Gambaro

Argentina

I am barely free to carry out fatal gestures.

Clarice Lispector

Griselda Gambaro.

Born in Buenos Aires, Argentina, 1928. Graduated from high school; began work in business office of publishing company, 1943; worked in business office of sports club, 1947–56. Married Juan Carlos Distéfano, a sculptor; traveled to Italy, 1955. Daughter Andrea born, 1961. Received National Endowment for the Arts prize to publish *Madrigal en ciudad,* 1963. Awarded the Emecé Publishers Prize for the collection of stories and short novels entitled *El desatino,* 1964. Son Lucas born, 1965. Received honorable mention in novel contest held by Sudamericana Publishers for *Una felicidad con menos pena,* 1967. Traveled to United States on International Exchange Program; won first prizes from Municipality of Buenos Aires, *Talía* magazine, and *Theatrical Broadcast News,* Municipal Radio of Buenos Aires, all for *El campo;* received Argentores Prize of Society of Argentinian Authors for *El campo,* 1968. Taught course on vanguard theater, University Extension Division, Universidad Nacional del Litoral, Argentina; traveled to Italy, 1969. Resided in Italy. Returned to Argentina, 1970. Traveled to United States for First International Drama Festival, San Francisco, 1972. Lecturer on theater today under auspices of the National Endowment for the Arts, 1973. Member of National Endowment for the Arts jury for annual national competitions, 1973–75. Traveled to Venezuela for Second International Drama Festival of Caracas, and then to France and Italy, 1974. Invited to France on occasion of publication of French translation of novel *Ganarse la muerte;* received Argentores Prize of Society of Argentinian Authors for "Sucede lo que pasa," 1976. *Ganarse la muerte* prohibited in Argentina; traveled to Spain; resided in Barcelona, 1977. Adapted *El campo* for Swedish radio; attended Third International Conference on Inter-American Women Writers in Ottawa, Canada; traveled to France for Symposium on Latin American Theatre organized by the Sorbonne and the Italian-Latin American Institute of Rome, 1978. Adapted *Los siameses* for French radio; traveled to United States for seminar on theater at Florida International University; guest lecturer at Yale, Cornell, Rice, Texas (Austin), and Arizona State universities, 1979. Returned to Argentina; traveled to Mexico for Fourth International Conference of Inter-American Women Authors, 1980. Awarded Guggenheim Fellowship; traveled to United States, Mexico, and France, 1982.

Although Griselda Gambaro is perhaps best known internationally for her dramatic works, she initiated her literary career with a prize-winning collection of short stories. She has recently returned to writing narrative fiction but continues her theatrical activities. Her concerns, however, are the same in both her novels and her plays: the image of mankind prevails in its more grotesque dimensions. Individual relationships and situations among friends, family, and acquaintances, as well as those that involve paternalistic societal and state institutions, reflect vividly and unabashedly man's inhumanity towards his fellow man. Under the guise of protectionism, the oppressor's insidious authoritarianism relies on the oppressed's passivity in order to isolate him and deprive him of his identity and liberty. For the most part, therefore, Gambaro's characters are either victimizers or the victimized. She depicts the interactions of these characters, which are dependent upon the submission and helplessness of the latter to the coldly calculated physical and psychic mutilation by the former.

Impotence, passivity, and suffering mark Gambaro's characters, as if life were lent to them and they had no hold on their destiny. Gambaro's protagonist the Écuyère explains: "Life is only a toy, Tristán, whose purpose we ignore except when it comes to challenging the unknown. We only possess a borrowed existence that we destroy as if it were ours for eternity, salvageable and infinite."[1] Gambaro's characters rarely experience the anguish, malaise, and self-reflection associated with much existentialist literature. Instead, they embody a nightmarish view of human relationships and their social and political implications. Only black humor relieves the tension produced by the author's grotesquely distorted and exaggerated portrayal of man's inhumanity. In her plays, she eschews sensationalism and emotionalism in the sadomasochistic situations by using slapstick, and in her novels, she assumes a distant narrative point of view delivered in a minor key. Still maintaining that subdued approach to monstrous cruelty, Gambaro only recently, in *Dios no nos quiere contentos* (God Doesn't Want Us to be Content), allowed an omniscient narrator to sympathize, albeit cynically, with her orphaned, battered progeny.

The juxtaposition of a dispassionate verbal system and a repugnant, menacing situation forms a cornerstone of duplicity in Gambaro's theater. The visual and dramatic impact of her plays relies heavily on the contradictions inherent in several forms of communication as she manipulates stage components—properties, costume design, make-up, movement, gestures, and off-stage sounds and smells—to contrast with dialogue. Gambaro's most powerful drama, *El campo (The Camp)*, perhaps best exemplifies this subtle interaction. The play's title refers variously to a bucolic setting in which children gambol in the fresh air, to a military installation, and to a concentration camp. These three environments are contrasted as children's voices and the songs of country folk are heard off-stage while Franco, one of the main characters, is dressed as an SS officer brandishing a whip onstage. He and his accountant Martin and a young woman named Emma form a sadomasochistic trinity in the play. Emma's physical appearance—she is barefoot, has a shaved head, wears a coarse gray smock, and displays a festering wounded hand and a face marked by long suffering—belies her smile and her delusion that she is festively attired and a famous pianist. She utters in a sophisticated tone, "What beautiful fingers! I'm a pianist!"[2]

All aspects of the play evoke the hypocrisy of a cruelty accepted passively by Emma and finally by Martin, her would-be saviour. She perceives Martin as an intruder in her relationship with her oppressor Franco, in her eyes her guardian. Even stage properties serve to falsify their function or physical nature, thus playing cruel jokes on the characters who try to use them. For example, one scene, a play-within-a-play episode, rivals a similar performance in Peter Weiss's drama *The Persecution and Assassination of Jean Paul Marat as Performed by the Inmates of the Asylum of Charenton under the Direction of the Marquis de Sade*. In the German play, the audience observes the inmates of the Charenton asylum as they enact their own play about the French Revolution before an audience of fellow lunatics. In *El campo* the audience is seated behind the last row of concentration camp inmates and SS guards assembled to hear a concert by a fellow prisoner, the pianist Emma, evoking what might be called "The Persecution of

Emma Represented by the Inmates of the Camp under the Direction of Franco." The props are flowers and a piano. Before the concert, Franco gives Emma a bouquet of artificial flowers; she sniffs them and exclaims, "How perfect!"[3] Although the piano does not function, she feigns the performance, accompanying the silence with a weak voice that is cruelly drowned out by the inmates who mock her and shout obscenities. Nevertheless, the most brutal actions are rendered innocuous in her delusion. In return for abuse, she praises her fellow prisoners as "charming people," a "select group of friends," and an adoring public. Her words are pathetic: "They would go crazy asking me for autographs; they ruined my shawl. . . . They almost destroyed me. . . . Completely."[4] As is typical of Gambaro's victims, Emma's passive reactions predominate: there is pain, rare flashes of anger, but never active rebellion or revenge.

The cruelty in *El campo* differs from that in other drama by Gambaro for the oppression in *El campo* transcends the individual situation to encompass the larger historical context explicitly portrayed in the Nazi uniforms; the mass destruction of individuals by divesting them of personality and abstracting them into faceless "Jews" or "Niggers" or "Communists"; the name Franco; and the smell of burning flesh (simulated off stage). The historical symbols of victimization in Gambaro's *El campo* attain legendary proportions, and, in that regard, approximate those of Antonin Artaud's theater of cruelty in which crime, love, war, and insanity were of little value in drama except to reveal the terrifying lyricism of the great myths that society accepted.

Gambaro's novel *Dios no nos quiere contentos* contains some of the characteristics of *El campo:* grotesque descriptions of the pathetic character of humankind's orphaned and abandoned beings; nightmarish episodes; and cruel and macabre relationships that illustrate the pervasive suffering and fatality. The narrative tone also depicts an almost matter-of-fact abnegation such as in the following passage about the girl María:

> She carried her pain like a burden, an internal hunchback never exposed to others, her road was different. Sticky and persistent, the pain adhered to her heart but she would not dignify it, would not call it anguish, melancholy or nostalgia, no great name for sadness, not even sadness. That it would be there,

inside, inevitable, because human beings and the world produced it like bees honey, flowers pollen, but she would never play the game of feeding it with her own compassion.[5]

Yet in this novel in which dialogue is sparse, new and important dimensions of Gambaro's world view emerge. The situations of the three primary characters are almost Kafkaesque: a young orphan boy, Tristán, whose sole desire is to sing, but he is unable to; the Écuyère, a contortionist and trapeze artist who works in a circus in which the owners continually mistreat her and move on to other towns, leaving her behind; and the babe, found by Tristán and the Écuyère on a crowded bus. The three live together, during which time Tristán has sexual adventures with his friend María in the whorehouse, the Écuyère is tied up and robbed by a vagabond she is infatuated with, and the babe, who grows up to support them all, fathers his own child and dies. In this world of macabre characterizations and oneiric scenes, Gambaro's poignant pronouncements on life's experiences surface like proverbs:

> No other destiny unites better than a shared expulsion from the same paradise; solitude fractured.

> Sometimes very little is left of man on this earth, barely a wound that someone carries about until he dies and then, nothing.

> Ah, what rotten humanity, she thought, as the ropes cut into her flesh without allowing her room to move, there is always someone more unfortunate who envies us.

> Words are nothing more than trappings, for that which we call the word exists in the depths prior to sound.[6]

Other "proverbs" approach such topics as solitude, human interactions, reality and dreams, happiness, love, perfection, and forgetfulness.

Despite these cynical philosophical reflections, Gambaro, in *Dios no nos quiere contentos,* for the first time offers her readers an energetic protagonist, victimized but active. The Écuyerè perceives the sadness and hypocrisy in man's unfathomable actions and yet in the circus of life, she maintains her identity. On her trapeze high above the crowd, she perfects her abilities so that the spectators below must recognize her existence. At the end of the novel, she lifts Tristán with her into the air and begins to sing; and so, too, finally, does Tristán, from whose lips emerge the meek strains of a lullaby, "freeing words from their subjugation to triviality and earth."[7]

Ottawa, Canada   *21 May 1978*

How did you become interested in the theater?

I don't remember. You see, when I was young I really didn't go to the theater; where I'm from, no one attended the theater very much. But I read a lot of Pirandello and O'Neill. Among some short narratives I once wrote, there was one called *Las paredes* [The Walls]—included in the book *El desatino* [The Blunder]—in which I felt I had not exhausted the theme. So I visualized the action into an image that was dramatic. The result was the play of the same name.

You didn't study drama in any formal way?

No, I simply have a dramatic intuition. You see, I completed five years of secondary education ["el bachillerato"] and then worked for two years for a publisher and later in business and accounting until I got married and my husband emancipated me.

You have published short stories, novels, and drama. How do you choose the appropriate genre?

I see certain themes visualized as drama. I write very few short stories, and lately I find a need to create novels. They allow for a type of introspection, or reflection, which differs from dramatic action.

When you say "themes" are you referring, for example, to the theme of violence or cruelty?

No, just to stories. I like to tell stories.

Do you consider yourself part of a specific generation of dramatists in Argentina?

No, I have remained rather isolated, even in Argentina. When my theater emerged in the midst of the Realistic School, I was attacked for my view of reality. Around 1965, I was opposed to the traditional "realism" in drama and still believe that each of us has his own voice; some "realistic" ones are excellent, but there are others that utilize parables and symbols to express another legitimate "reality."

Did the public and the critics find your plays difficult to accept?

There had been others like mine before, and some critics supported me while others rejected me outright.

Are Argentinians great theatergoers?

There is a good following. But the public has trouble accepting me. I'm not a popular author, although strangely enough, Argentina is a country steeped in the grotesque, in grotesque theater. In my experience, nevertheless, with certain plays like "Nada que ver" [It's Not So] in which ridicule and comedy interact, people seem compelled to reject the play strongly. If they laugh they want to do so wholeheartedly, or if they cry they wish to do so frankly. But the mixture of the two sentiments disconcerts them.

Do you think the grotesque element also upsets them?

Yes, the themes are somewhat cruel, aren't they?

Yes.

They are not very gratifying.

Not at all. Do you have both commercial theater and experimental theater in Argentina?

Yes, but our experimental theater does not stage productions in the universities as in your country.

What are the principal aesthetic influences on your narrative and drama?

It would be difficult to say because I'm not a very organized reader. For example, sometimes I read a detective story and suddenly feel it stir something within me, whereas the most marvelous book may not offer me anything of value. What is intellectual or literary often opens small doors or windows onto my own fiction and helps me to formulate it. But, in general, life experiences motivate me to write—what one lives, sees, gathers together, and suffers.

61

Do you yourself go to the theater a lot?

No. In Argentina I never used to see much theater because when drama is bad it's unbearable. And I have less patience each time.

You spoke of the importance of life experiences. Have any influenced you more than others?

No, but of course the fact that I am now living in Barcelona is an experience which I have been able to incorporate into the novel I am writing. You know, the creative process is quite complex. There may be some writers motivated by blind revelation who sit down and write, but for me it is a slow, sensitive, intellectual, and emotional process. It requires time and maturity. The Uruguayan Felisberto Hernández once said that at a certain moment he would feel a tiny plant take root within him, but he did not know how the plant would grow, or if it would be hardy. He knew only that he had to care for it. Those are not his exact words but that is how it feels to me, also. I know something has been born.

Have you ever taught drama?

No, I've never taught, and it's a shame because I think that would involve me in a more active way with people. One ends up accepting the solitude of a writer.

Can you earn a living as an author?

No. Not at all.

What work do you do, then?

Domestic labor. My husband supports us financially; sometimes I am able to help a little. And I contribute by tending to the home even though I don't like that type of work.

Is he also a writer?

No, no competition, please. He's a sculptor who, at times, gives me his opinion of my manuscripts. I respect that advice.

As a sculptor he also has an artistic sensitivity.

Yes, a certain life-style, a goal to create a work. So we have common interests; but also, we coincide in practical matters such as schedules and discipline. Our mornings are sacred. We rise early. I am very disciplined in my work because I have no excess time to spare.

Most critics seem to categorize your drama as theater of the absurd or theater of cruelty. Do you agree?

First of all, I despise neat cubbyholes even though they may aid the critics. But I don't think theater of the absurd is accurate. I deal with real facts; it's just that my form of expression isn't realistic.

Besides, in the theater of the absurd an unexplained anguish or "absurdity" always remains, never totally defined in "realistic" terms, whereas in your drama, one can decipher the symbols within a real context, perhaps on many levels.

Exactly. There are many facets to reality. That is precisely where the realists err, in the belief that a single valid level of reality lies in a photographic transcription. But there are multiple levels, some visible or invisible or subterranean.

Your theater usually communicates several specific messages.

There is often an implicit ethical intent. A play like *El campo* is transparent and cannot be classified as absurd.

To me El campo *leans much more in the direction of the theater of cruelty for, as Antonin Artaud proposed, you provoke the audience so it can neither identify with nor reject the action but rather experience it, feel it, and not just intellectualize it. Words and action communicate scenes of horror or cruelty that shock the public so that it will not perpetrate such cruelty outside the theater in its own world.*

The text of *El campo* is very important because the situations are based on a tension between words and deeds.

Yes, a duplicity. One critic has pointed out the importance of the action and not the words in El campo. *I don't agree. In fact, what is most important in* El campo *is the relationship between words and the other characteristics of drama: action, props, scenery, costumes, make-up, noises, and smells both on and off stage. Words almost always contradict the visual reality; therefore, words are important.*

Besides, in *El campo* the negated words comprise the action itself.

In most of your work one man's freedom is circumscribed by another's. Man doesn't enjoy freedom nor does he fight to cast off his slavery.

Well, one can change, and I feel that in the last two years I have emerged from that mold. For example, in "Cada cosa en su lugar" [Everything in Its Place; to date unpublished] the female protagonist actively chooses her own options. I could not bring myself to create another character who would suffer as much as the protagonist in the novel *Ganarse la muerte* [To Earn Death]. One often has a single theme, and I probably have mine, the problem of passivity. It must be due to personal reasons; I am a very cowardly woman.

In what way?

Very cowardly in every way. I'm not brave; I find it difficult to be brave. I am very preoccupied with passivity and the nonassumption of individual responsibility. In society it is that way and, also, in my plays. Perhaps I have altered that view somewhat now. It is less bitter only on the human level but not on the political one, or the social one.

In your work, children are often as cruel as adults, as cruel as some of the children who inhabit short stories by Silvina Ocampo.

But I think children are inherently innocent so that when they are cruel it is not the same as when an adult is cruel.

Because a child's cruelty is not premeditated or because he has no ethical basis?

It may be premeditated but I find him much more innocent. It's a shame I can't give you some examples from my book *Conversaciones con Chicos* [Conversing with Children]; I haven't a copy left.

And what about man's inhumanity to man, the adults in your plays, for instance in El campo?

There it's the memories of Nazi concentration camps, of a society's distorted values. Our history is very painful. One has only to read the newspapers.

Are you saying that cruelty springs forth from a social and political context, a historical reality, and not because you believe that individuals are innately cruel?

It's difficult to say. Many are capable of good and evil, historically. I am amazed at man's capacity for altruism and also for indescribable depravity. And that evil always seems to weigh on me. I feel out of step with a world of political slogans where in the end some poor creature is battered and destroyed.

It is precisely in El campo *that this collective cruelty seems to emerge.*
Yes, and each time I draw closer to that interpretation, a less personal one. In the other plays, I portrayed a more or less individual cruelty.

Is man more capable of cruelty as an individual or in a group?
All great catastrophes have been undertaken by collectivities. But at the same time we need to unite because individuals carry little weight in this society. However, we always unite for a lost cause, wars, hecatombs. The advantages we now enjoy were achieved by people who fought for them in the past during a slow process. We are menaced now by unpredictable disasters, such as the proliferation of armaments. We live in a society that seems tranquil and peaceful, but it is really terrible to measure the threat that we have become accustomed to and have accepted.

Your characters reflect these undercurrents of terror. Their smiles almost always belie pain and fear. Why do you insist on this contradiction—the smile that hides cruelty?
Even though *El desatino,* for example, may be a cruel play, the action is humorous. When it played in Buenos Aires it was very entertaining and funny. A kind of macabre humor. *Los siameses* [The Siamese Twins] had the same comic effect, although, when it was translated into French, it impressed the French people as a very painful play. But in Buenos Aires they received it with laughter, until the closing scene.

You meant it to be humorous?
No, but it turned out that way because it was amusing and the character was ingenuous. In my last novel, *Ganarse la muerte,* a similar atmosphere exists. Of course, the situations are so ghastly that few saw humor in the language, blinded as they were by the impact of the story. I tried to relate horrors by means of humor.

I must confess that the humor in your works is lost on me. I believe that there is a very fine line between comedy and tragedy in your plays, and so an actor or actress could easily play a part too melodramatically or in too slapstick a fashion, like a clown. The balance must be maintained.

Curiously enough, the best performances have been by actors who live the character and indentify with him from the very first reading.

Only the novel Una felicidad con menos pena *(Happiness with Less Sorrow) made me laugh, and the play "Nada que ver," a little bit. In the text or script, the humor, as you call it, of the performance is lost. And so for you the intention is humorous?*

Yes. Of course, it is black humor, which some reject.

Exactly. The humor in Una felicidad con menos pena *is based on the grotesque.*

Yes, it evokes that atmosphere. Humor is provoked by the exaggerated accentuation of certain details.

What can you tell me about the genesis of that short novel, the absurd situation in which the characters find themselves, the grotesque view of that room heaped with people?

I cannot recall. It was so long ago.

Let's return then to a more recent work, the play El campo. *I see in it various possible levels of interpretation: the individual as the victim of cruelty; society that classifies us and marks us for persecution (as Communists or Jews, whatever); and the political power of a tyrant whose cruelty is masked behind his pose as a benefactor.*

Yes, it is so, even though I didn't deliberately think in those terms. Also, there are other facets: Emma's passivity, Martin's acceptance of the situation, the lack of identity.

Are all these interpretations equally important?

That depends. A sensitive public captures that sensitivity, a more intellectual public is attentive to an intellectual significance. A work functions as a totality. If one wishes to accentuate one aspect or another, that's legitimate. As for my creativity, I am not very rational. I proceed on a more sensitive level and use my intellect to support my feelings. If one is to master writing, to polish and perfect a style, the work itself provides the means to do so. Constant work hones your tools. Some writers begin with an intellectual or ideological premise. It's very dangerous to use an ideological premise. I do not.

Which Latin American writers interest you?

The Chilean José Donoso. The Spaniard Juan Marsé. I like Cortázar although his world is not mine. But I like *Historias de cronopios y de famas* [*Cronopios and Famas*] and his short stories in *Bestiario* [Bestiary].

And what of your favorite dramatists nowadays?

From Argentina? They're unknown, underground writers like Adellach, Gallipoli, González Arquati, and Serebrinsky.

What type of drama do they produce?

Mostly about repulsive themes like staged pregnancies and births. But I find a certain passion and vision in those playwrights.

What is your opinion of Latin American theater in general?

Theater is a social, collective phenomenon. It is related, therefore, to what is occurring in each country. If a country is experiencing a crisis, the theater reflects that immediately. Unlike the novel that you can write at home and publish some years later, the theater is public and presents other problems that are linked to a social or political domain.

Do you consider the drama of certain countries to be better than others?

You know, we are very isolated from each other. We know very little about what's going on in Chile, for instance. We infrequently receive books from other Latin American countries and so we look towards Europe and know the latest from across the sea. There is a great lack of communication.

Which women authors from the past are most important in your view?

Gabriela Mistral, Juana de Ibarbourou, Delmira Agustini, Alfonsina Storni. Although I confess I feel somewhat removed from them, as if in another dimension of time.

And women writers today?

The Argentinian poet Olga Orozco who has written a lyrical novel *La oscuridad es otro sol* [Darkness Is Another Sun], and Alejandra Pizarnik. I also feel close to the Brazilian Clarice Lispector.

Do women authors deal with some themes differently than male authors? Is there such a thing as feminine or masculine literature?

Mercedes Valdivieso believes that feminine literature is discernible through the relationships between characters. It is a wise observation. Women *do* have a certain view that expresses itself through those relationships. I have no exhaustive evidence to support this idea. I would have to read more, undertake some research. But I feel the principle to be sound. However, I refuse to write "like a woman." It comes naturally, one doesn't think about it; one simply is a woman and doesn't write like a man.

How does a woman author fare in Latin America?

Almost the same way as a man. I speak of Argentina, of course. I don't think there are restrictions on men or women writers. The proof lies in the quantity of women novelists we have in Argentina—apart from quality—who write best-sellers. The problems reside with the individual as a commercial success. But if one attempts a critical view of society, the doors shut you out, whether you're a man or a woman. In my case, at least, I don't believe I've been limited because of my sex. But I'm not very competitive. It's difficult for me to visit a publisher and push my books. You have to mobilize yourself to attain something. I suppose it's my work that takes up all of my time. So when I have to do something "social" or practical, it's terrible. I'm so insecure at times that I need to bolster myself. I think it has to do more with social class than with sex. All the successful women in Argentina have been from the upper class, like Luisa Mercedes Levinson, Marta Lynch, Silvina Ocampo, Elvira Orphée. Their social stature provides them with a sense of security rooted in a childhood without want for material needs.

And your childhood?

I'm from Buenos Aires, but from a different class. My father worked in the post office. I'm from a poor family. Now things are much better but that circumstance marks you forever. I remember how much I wanted to learn English when I was young. But studying was a sacrifice; I went at night to inferior public schools and learned nothing. I ask myself whether or not I might have gone to the best English school, if I'd been born in another class.

What are you writing now?

A novel called *Dios no nos quiere contentos.* It's like the popular saying "Dios no quiere contentos," which seemed so terrible to me. The action centers on trivial events. It's the story of a trapeze artist, the Écuyère, who is really a contortionist capable of twisting herself into knots. She works in a circus that's constantly moving away from her. Although she is always abandoned by the circus, where the owners exploit her, she pursues it wherever it goes. She cannot live without it. Her search is interwoven with the story of a young boy who wants to sing. Only at the very end of the novel does he emit a mournful noise. The Écuyère and the boy come across a lost child while they are riding a bus so packed with people that the contortionist has to hang herself in a knot from the roof of the vehicle during a very comical but cruel scene. Since none offers to get up and give his seat to the mother, the poor little child strays from her arms and is passed from one passenger to another. He cries with some young girls, he pulls an old man's beard, and finally is lost in the crowd. When the Écuyère gets off the bus and unwinds herself, the small child falls from her arms to the ground and comes to live with her and the boy. Many strange things happen to these three characters, but I believe the conclusion is optimistic, even though my husband says it's very sad. You see, at the end, the Écuyère concludes that from her trapeze above the earth she cannot be an embittered creature. There are many themes in this novel: a feeling of being lost far from my country; the circus is my country to some extent. So I'm content for I've breathed fresh air at a distance; that has been beneficial to me.

Does the situation of the female author in Spanish America differ from that of the male author? Does she have the same opportunities to pub-

*lish her work and to circulate it in her own country? Abroad? In transla-
tions? The same opportunities to win national or international literary
prizes?*

I don't know enough about the situation in other Latin American
countries to give my opinion. As far as Argentina, or specifically Buenos Aires, is concerned, I don't believe that the female author's situation is very different from the male's. The same goes for translations
and international renown. They are both faced with the same difficul-
ties concerning publication, nationally due to the economic crisis and
abroad because of the relative disregard for our literature. I'm unaware of how international prizes are bestowed on a writer but with
regard to Argentina I could all but assure you that no discrimination
exists whatsoever.

*Are there certain taboo themes for women writers that would be ac-
cepted more easily by society if the author were a man?*

Of course, society accepts certain themes much more easily when a
male author deals with them. If women had written what Henry Miller
or Jean Genet has, a doubly provocative scandal would have broken
out. On the other hand, I don't think there are any real taboo subjects
for women; it all depends on individual courage and authority.

*In your fiction, do you consciously or subconsciously broach themes
that specifically pertain to the Spanish American woman? Are you concerned with woman's socioeconomic role in Spanish America?*

I suppose that in my fiction I broach themes that pertain to women,
but not deliberately. My life experience is that of a woman, a Spanish
American woman, and my themes are unavoidably filtered through
that circumstance.

*Recently, have you been able to earn a living exclusively by writing
fiction?*

During these last few years, I could have lived by writing fiction. In
1982 I received a Guggenheim, and in addition to my royalties as a
novelist, I add my even more important rights as a dramatist and my
earnings for collaborating in other media.

*What are you writing now? Does it sustain your interests expressed in
earlier works? Are there new experiments, directions?*

Each work presents me with a new set of problems, as if I'd never produced fiction before, whether novel or drama. While a work is in gestation, before the actual writing process, I don't know what form it will take. Right now I'm preparing a collection of short stories.

Presently, what kind of readings interest you most?
The same as always: first novels, then poetry and drama.

There are many Spanish American writers who do not live or have not lived at some time in their own countries but rather have written from abroad—for political, social, or personal reasons—in voluntary or involuntary exile: Cortázar, García Márquez, Vargas Llosa, Puig, Donoso. Does this situation apply to women writers from Spanish America? Do they feel the need or desire to distance themselves from their social context? Can they do so as easily as male authors?
I can only speak for the Argentinian woman. I don't believe she feels the need to distance herself from her country except in extreme political circumstances that have occurred at times. Presently, she is very committed to, and increasingly integrated into, her surroundings (María Elena Walsh, Marta Mercader, Angélica Gorodischer, Libertad Demitropulos, Noemí Ulla).

Since we met for the interview, have you written other books? Would you describe the importance you attach to your recently published fiction?
I'm not sure of the importance one should attribute to my last novel, *Dios no nos quiere contentos.* I can only say that in that book I develop my characters in a new way, with a more tender, comprehensive attitude. Technically, the novel's structure is more complex than that of my earlier works. Furthermore, in *Dios no nos quiere contentos,* as in "La Malasangre" [Bad Blood] (the latest play performed in Buenos Aires), there is a search for an answer in which I, the author, am implicated; I allow myself to reflect with my own voice among my characters.

Julieta Campos

Cuba, Mexico

I am creating myself. And we walk in complete darkness in search of ourselves. It hurts. But it is the pain of childbirth: something is born. It exists.

Clarice Lispector

Julieta Campos. (Photo Paulina Lavista.)

Born in Havana, Cuba, 1932. Earned B.A., University of Havana, 1952. Received scholarship from Alliance Française to study in Paris, 1953. Received certificate in contemporary french literature, Sorbonne, Paris; traveled throughout Italy; married Mexican Enrique González Pedrero in Paris, 1954. Earned Ph.D., University of Havana; son Emiliano born; moved to Mexico City, 1955. Collaborator on magazines and cultural supplements, 1956–64. Translator of English and French into Spanish; has translated approximately thirty-eight books about the social sciences, history, and psychoanalysis, 1958—. Mother died in Havana, 1964. Traveled to Buenos Aires and Lima, 1966. Received grant from Center for Mexican Writers to write *Celina o los gatos,* 1967. Traveled to Germany, 1969. Traveled to France, Switzerland, Italy, Spain, Greece, United States, Canada, and various Caribbean islands, 1971–76. Won Xavier Villaurrutia Prize for novel *Tiene los cabellos rojizos y se llama Sabina;* collaborator on magazine *Plural,* edited by Octavio Paz, 1975. Attended Second International Conference on Inter-American Women Authors, San Jose, California; visited Anaïs Nin in Los Angeles; taught literature at National Institute of Public Education, Acatlán, National Autonomous University of Mexico, 1976. Collaborator and member of editorial board of *Vuelta,* 1977—. Attended Third International Conference on Inter-American Women Authors, Ottawa, Canada; elected president of P.E.N. Club of Mexico, 1978. Became editor of *Revista de la Universidad de México,* 1981. Resides both in Mexico City, Mexico, and in Villahermosa, Tabasco, Mexico, where husband is governor, 1982—.

Fiction for Julieta Campos marks the apotheosis of a writing that fills the irreproachable and silent void caused by two existential fatalities: love (Eros) and death (Thanatos). In her essays on literary theory collected in *La imagen en el espejo* (The Mirror's Eye) and *Función de la novela* (The Novel's Function), Campos has provided us with the keys to her own narrative. She notes that writing "never knows what it is seeking, ignores what it has to say; it is invention, the invention of the world and of man, constant invention and perpetual challenge."[1] Concerning the irreproachable void, she discloses, "I always knew, secretly, that writing was a way of filling what I kept on experiencing as a void, despite all the true gratifications of real life."[2] And furthermore, she compares writing to the attempt of Orpheus to save Eurydice, the object of his love, from death: "Faithful to the urgent need to bring to light the obscure object of that desire, Orpheus reclaims Eurydice every time a text emerges from silence."[3] Campos's novels are an attempt to confront with art the inadequacies of life. They are a means of facing personal crises such as illness, of exorcising feelings about the nature of time and death, and of inhabiting the interstices of a reality rent by her aspirations for something more than the world can offer.[4]

Muerte por agua (Death by Water), her first novel, published in its third and definitive version in 1978, was a reaction to her mother's bout with cancer, an attempt to fill with words the distance that separated mother and daughter living in different countries. In *Muerte por agua* Campos established several constants in her narrative style and discovered a few points of contact with the French "new novel." In her intimate and detailed narrative the constants that emerge are a minimal plot; imperceptible physical motion; the failure of the characters to act decisively; the characters' sensitivity and great receptivity to internal voices of conscience and to their surroundings, which are sharply contrasted with the banal conversations sustained between them; their self-reflexive natures circumscribed by a specific physical setting; situations and thoughts devoid of logical relations to each other which, as a result, force the reader to supply the missing links; time as a corrosive element—symbolized by water, rain, termites, and even man-eating plants—that dilutes, devours, invades, and finally takes possession of city, house, body; and the presence of blinding light, ships and shipwrecks on the high seas, shells, paintings, and photographs. In connection with the French "new novel," *Muerte por agua* features the similar protagonist-narrator who subjectively selects and obsessively zeroes in on certain objects; the absence of the dynamics inherent in a traditional plot; and, above all, a subliminal dialogue similar to that found in Nathalie Sarraute's novels, like "a muted battle in which a true sense of life and death vie to emerge amidst commonplaces."[5]

It appears that these links between Campos's first novel and the French "new novel" have led some critics astray in their judgment of her second novel, *Tiene los cabellos rojizos y se llama Sabina* (A Redhead Named Sabina), a work in which an artist depicts herself during the creative process and renders a work similar to Velázquez's painting *Las Meninas* (1656) and Picasso's *Carnets de la Californie* (1955). Campos has also dealt with this theme in her literary criticism, which encompasses studies on such varied subjects as Ernest Hemingway, Virginia Woolf, Michel Butor, Simone de Beauvoir, Sarraute, Alain Robbe-Grillet, Alejo Carpentier, Juan Rulfo, and Agustín Yáñez. Self-reflexive writing as a theme links *Sabina* to its Hispanic roots in *Don Quijote de la Mancha* and to a modern tradition in Europe and Spanish America embodied in Gide's *Les Faux-Monnayeurs (The Counterfeiters),* Claude Mauriac's *L'agrandissement* (Expansion), Sarraute's *Les Fruits d'or (Golden Fruits)* and Salvador Elizondo's *El hipogeo secreto* (The Secret Catacombs).

However, *Sabina's* outstanding accomplishment does not lie in the exploration of its own genesis but rather in its fusion of theme and novelistic structure, a unified, defiant challenge to the inexorable flow of time in the novel, which progresses towards no conclusive outcome. Campos explains that "the obsessive usury of time has always troubled me, the annihilation of human life and of objects, forgetfulness. . . . A conscious state in self contemplation inevitably ends up running across the image of death."[6] *Sabina's* greatest merit is, therefore, its narrative structure, at once the search for and the solution to the problem of mortality.

A decade prior to the publication of *Sabina,* the Argentinian Julio Cortázar had written *Rayuela (Hopscotch)* in which one of the characters, Morelli, had presented some daring and unconventional theories about writing antinovels, ideas which Cortázar himself experimented with in 1968 in his novel *62: Modelo para armar (62: A Model Kit).* Cortázar's "morelliana" describes the atmosphere of such an antinovel, one which Campos was to achieve successfully in *Sabina.* He notes that in his "actors" (characters in the novel), "something which Homo sapiens keeps subliminal would laboriously open up a road as if a third eye were blinking out with effort from under the frontal bone. Everything would be a kind of disquiet, a continuous uprooting, a territory where psychological causality would yield disconcertedly."[7]

Novelistic structures which create an atmosphere of simultaneity abound in contemporary Spanish American fiction, in part as a result of the truncated forms of prose prevalent in the beginning of the twentieth-century vanguard period: the possible reading of *Rayuela* as a collage of chapters, the montage of plots in Mario Vargas Llosa's *La casa verde (The Green House),* the gallery of voices in Guillermo Cabrera Infante's *Tres tristes tigres (Three Trapped Tigers),* or the scenic duality of Salvador Elizondo's *Farabeuf (Farabeuf).* In them logical transitions between episodes disappear or are hidden, voids are created, and information is deferred in order to goad the reader into participating in the reconstruction of a fragmented plot. The incomplete structures produce puzzles which the reader must piece together. Nevertheless, in the aforementioned novels, text and texture do not usually form a unified focus since the disjointed framework of those novels generally serves only as a scaffolding for their various themes, not as the theme itself. Although, in different degrees, they all exhibit characteristics of the "open work" defined by Umberto Eco,[8] and their complexities can ultimately be unraveled by the reader into understandable resolutions.

None of these novels achieves success as an "open work," replete with ambiguities and contradictions, to the extent that *Sabina* does in its constant metamorphosis. Plural meanings emerge in an unceasing dialogue sustained by author, text, and reader. *Sabina's* polysemous structure seems to defy reorganization into ordered, sequential episodes in time, thus denying the reader a traditional plot and a traditional reading. In doing this, Campos challenges the flow of time toward forgetfulness, toward the novel's end, toward the deaths of the protagonists. The entire novel takes place during the moment the main character, Sabina, looks out at the sea at five o'clock in the afternoon on the last day of her vacation in Acapulco.

While the steady, slow rhythm of the rain in *Muerte por agua* emphasizes the successive and unbearable plodding of time victorious, *Sabina* is a spell conjured against time. By unleashing an unceasing and implacable flood of memories, hopes, mirages, and fantasies, Campos attempts to meet and hold off the inexorable flow of time. The closed spaces—city, house, garden—of the short stories in *Celina o los gatos* (Celina or the Cats) explode in *Sabina* into magical realms of imagination and creativity shaped by the multiple meanings of a text which Campos describes as "a propitious meeting place of confluent magnetism."[9]

In Campos's novel *El miedo de perder a Eurídice* (Fear of Losing Eurydice), water continues to prevail as a "two-edged symbol: at once, life and death."[10] As in *Sabina,* the absence of a plot and the presence of an immobilized protagonist persist in *Eurídice:* a professor of French, seated at the Palace of Minos café in Mexico, reads a novel by Jules Verne, draws an island on a napkin, dreams of adventures and shipwrecks, and writes a diary that coincides with a love story. "Everything that happens, happens as he waits there, at the moment when writing comes between fantasy and reality."[11] In *Eurídice* that moment becomes populated almost exclusively with the artistic heritage of Western cultures. The title, for instance, refers to the Greek myth of Orpheus, who tried to save his wife Eurydice, from death. In the novel, Campos, like Orpheus, attempts to recover love from death by spinning constant literary re-presentations of the primordial utopia, of the original paradisiacal love between Eve and Adam. The amorous encounters—sometimes beautifully erotic, other times simply mechanical—challenge time and annihilate the routine and boredom into which love and desire often fade. The novel salvages and isolates lovers from time immemorial "in a verbal object, an image, that obscure object of desire that Orpheus tried to wrench from the darkness incarnated in the person of Eurydice."[12]

El miedo de perder a Eurídice sublimates human love; art rescues love from death. The novel is the desire, the eternal search for a utopia, transformed into writing about writing and, by extension, about Western cultures: art, drama, opera, film, music, geography, philosophy, and, above all, literature. The many references to cultural phenomena in *Sabina* and especially in *El miedo de perder a Eurídice* are reminiscent of Campos's workshop, a room overflowing with books, paintings, photographs, feline-shaped pillows, and shells. Every now and then, among these objects, one can hear the muffled sounds of one of her five cats, perhaps the mother cat, Clarissa Dalloway.

I'd like to know just how you began to write fiction.

My mother was slowly dying of lung cancer. We had been living far from each other in different cities and countries for some years then. But the imminence of death transformed that distance into the most anguishing emptiness that I had ever experienced up to that time. I wrote to fill that void; and so *Muerte por agua* began to take shape within me. I finished two completely different versions before the definitive one to be entitled *Sus mamparas siempre están cerradas* [Behind Closed Shutters] or *Una partida de brisca* [The Card Game]. The title *Muerte por agua* was a compromise with the publisher. It obviously comes from T. S. Eliot. In a future edition, I'd like to change the title. Perhaps I might call it *Naturaleza muerta* [Still Life] or *Retrato de familia en un interior en el trópico* [Family Portrait in the Tropics]. Since that first novel, I understood that for me writing fiction compensated for a loss; it has always been so, a kind of exorcism, a way of ridding myself of something that I must put into words.

Yet even though such exorcisms occur, certain themes seem to reappear in your fiction.

Yes. I don't think one ever completely frees oneself of them. A writer's stock is like Ariadne's thread or the crumbs that Gretel dropped in the forest. So one doesn't overcome themes, but rather always crystalizes them incompletely.

I like the Ariadne image and the labyrinth.

I believe that all books are labyrinths in which one reaches the center, the place where the fight with the Minotaur takes place. And if the book is well-written, then Theseus emerges victorious; if not, the Minotaur does.

Are you more at ease with the novelistic form or the short story?

I don't believe I know how to write short stories, traditionally speaking, short stories with unexpected endings. I've never created such stories; mine tend to be lengthy discourses with a novelistic rhythm. They do not possess the economy or synthesis that the classical short story requires. Actually, I have never been concerned with that problem. My texts cannot be classified by traditional genre standards, for more and more they are a written form that encompasses all genres—essay, poetry, narrative, criticism, drama.

What relationship do you see between your profession as a literary critic and that of a writer of fiction?

For years I swung like a pendulum with a rather constant rhythm between my other work and my fiction. Now my reflexive and critical discourse and my fiction slide so imperceptibly by each other that it is difficult to separate or distinguish them. Don't you think it seems so in *Tiene los cabellos rojizos y se llama Sabina?* The writing and its criticism comprise a single text: a weaving in which strange voices and other works converge, incorporated within me so that I felt them to be my own. Each time, my criticism is less isolated from narrative forms in a kind of symbiosis between criticism and fiction.

In Muerte por agua, *the interior dialogue that each character sustains within himself seems similar to the ones that Nathalie Sarraute utilizes in her novels. Has her narrative had an influence on yours?*

I believe that we always have many influences, some conscious, others unconscious, and that some texts often deliberately impinge on a particular writer's work. Writing stems from an unconscious level. Just as we fabricate dreams while asleep, we conceive books while awake. It is a comparable process in which the impulse or motivation originates in the unconscious where, at times, certain influences assimilated over time accumulate and remain unnoticed during the writing experience. Nevertheless, they persist. I had read a lot of Nathalie Sarraute's fiction before I wrote *Muerte por agua.* For many years now I have not read the so-called French "new novel." But I probably was influenced somewhat by Nathalie Sarraute. Not in a consciously imitated style, though she must have been there in spirit along with Virginia Woolf.

The anguished immobility of Muerte por agua *appears to have a counterpart in* Tiene los cabellos rojizos y se llama Sabina *where that immobility is vitalized. I would call* Muerte por agua *a pessimistic novel; whereas, to me,* Sabina *is optimistic.*

I don't know if *Sabina* is optimistic. Clearly, one great contrast exists in the utilization of space. In *Muerte por agua,* space is closed, inward; the three characters are islands unto themselves, circumscribed by the equally insular space of a house surrounded on all sides by water, a house on an island also encircled by water. That space deteriorates and decays. *Sabina*'s space is open. Sabina is a character situated precisely in an open place, on an immensely open vantage point facing the sea. For the first time in my work, the character abandons the confines of a house and exposes herself to the world, to a view of that sea that evokes so much outside of the closed space where my characters had always moved.

What about the two dates at the end of the novel: 1971 in Acapulco and 1973 in Cuernavaca?

They are the dates when I began and finished the novel. I only wrote the last few pages in Cuernavaca. All the rest was written in Mexico City with the exception of a few parts in Acapulco.

And you began in 1971 and finished about two years later?

Yes, because for many months I wrote nothing and, then, suddenly took up the thread again. . . . As opposed to my first novel, *Sabina* was born in its first and decisive shape. It was barely corrected, hardly altered from the original.

Speaking about dates, they proliferate in Sabina. *You're always referring to explorers, for example, or to a time "twenty-two years ago." Why do you insist on exact dates?*

I feel that a text like *Sabina* responds to the author's design to rescue time from its flux, from its journey into death, by trying to detain a portion of that time that eludes us. The dates serve that end; they wrest time in the book and rescue the book from death.

The novel begins with, "I am not here, I am on another beach twenty-two years ago."

I have placed the character in a specific place, and, at the same time, she is in many other imaginary spaces. I was suggesting to the reader that the character is there but also in time-gone-by and time-to-come. She experiences both her memories and her anticipations of a different life. At that specific moment, her entire life experience converges.

You carry off a kind of game in Sabina. *You play with the reader, the critic, even the novel itself.*

Writing is always a game.

But in Muerte por agua *that element is absent.*

Perhaps so. But more and more I feel that writing is a game. The very idea of proposing a totally fictitious reality to a reader in order to make him believe it is true, *that* is a game.

But you don't allow the reader to deceive himself.

No, on the contrary.

Before discussing Sabina *any further, I'd like to hear about your literary interests and about any influences on your own fiction.*

Right now, I'm reading books about the Kabbala, alchemy, magic, the occult, and a fascinating history of the labyrinth as myth and symbol; not because I'm writing a book about them but because I feel somehow that I need to incorporate them into me so that they may emerge in my book. In search of profound affinities, I read the *Archipelago* by Hölderlin, too, a long poem that forms part of my interest in German Romanticism. Also the very beautiful text by the Chilean Rosamel del Valle called *Eva y la fuga* [Eve and Flight], written two years after *Nadja* by Breton, has come to be the quintessence in Spanish of the spirit in which *Nadja* was conceived. I should mention that now I am writing a book that will perhaps be called *La pérdida de Eurídice* [Eurydice Lost], dedicated "to the memory of Nadja." This explains the enthusiasm and completely exaggerated emotion with which I have read *Eva y la fuga*. At this moment all of these books revolve within an orbit circumscribed by the text I am working on concerned with the myth of the couple and the myth of the island. As for labyrinths, all those imagined in Western culture find their remote origin in one island—Crete, of course.

And influences on your fiction?

I'd rather have you uncover them and describe them to me. It would be much more amusing and certainly more accurate.

In what kind of atmosphere do you prefer to write—with music, cats, in colored inks?

My ideal setting would be that of *Sabina,* on a terrace overlooking the sea. I hope to be able to do that some day. However, since that is impossible now, I usually write in my study, which as you see is very small, filled with books and all sorts of cats—live and in ceramic or cloth, sketched, and painted—and I listen to music.

A certain kind?

I can listen to jazz; it depends on what I'm writing. But, generally, I listen to Baroque music and Wagner or Chopin. Right now I prefer the Romantics because of what I'm writing. I hardly ever work in total silence. Perhaps due to the level of noise from the street, I use music like a screen between the street racket and myself.

And if you were seated facing the sea?

If I had the sea, I wouldn't need any other music. To me it is the perfect music.

In Función de la novela *you emphasize the selection and relationship of situations. Applying those criteria to* Sabina, *would you explain the process?*

I believe that the method was similar to that of free association in psychoanalysis. Sabina is a multiple character who gathers together levels of experience that in reality remain fragmented and dispersed. Sabina's imaginary nature allows me to bring about a coincidence in her of realities and fantasies that real life would not have synthesized. In the fictitious realm, what has actually happened does not occur but rather what could have happened, occurs: situations and events finally find their most profound logic by coalescing through the organization of words in a privileged and imaginary space.

There seem to be two types of plots in Sabina: *one that unravels in the hotel where so many undeveloped characters enter and exit—the play-*

boy, the Englishman—and create suspenseful truncated plots related in some way to the danger felt by the protagonist. In addition, there is another kind of oneiric series of dangerous plots—about suicides and madness—ones that are never fully developed either. Nevertheless, they are more important, poignant, and intimate.

I believe that some episodes and characters are grouped, we might say, into minor ones on a secondary level, like the background in a painting or extras in a movie. The people at the hotel play that role. The protagonist watches them simply because they are there as suggestive catalysts for the imagination to associate with other memories, invented characters, and autobiographic incidents. A writer senses stimuli in reality—perceptions, sensations, themes—and connects them, as if in a dream. After all, dreams are real, so is fantasy.

In La imagen en el espejo *you explain how the mirror does not reflect a true image.*

It reflects that image and something beyond, precisely the way literature captures reality.

In your narrative, especially in Sabina, *a parallel emerges between objects corroded by sea salt and illness that slowly destroys your characters.*

You are right, a preoccupation with sickness is reiterated throughout my books. Now that you have made me aware of it, I associate its origins with my mother's illness from the very first novel. Sickness is only a surreptitious manifestation of the corrosion of life that sweeps humanity and things towards disintegration and death. Signs of this obsession often appear in my work: the termite that bores holes in the furniture in *Muerte por agua* and the rain that blurs limits and dilutes characters in an anguished symbiotic indifference; Celina's mysterious illness personified by the cats; the disease that attacks the roses, invades the house, and manifests itself in the character's madness in "Todas las rosas" [All the Roses]. In fact, the corrosive nature of the sea is a sensitive and obvious manifestation of time devouring our lives. Sickness interests me, to the extent that it allows a more intense spiritual organization to emerge from within the deteriorating body. That is, I am attracted by the romantic notion of illness. I explore how and why mysterious paths sometimes nurture a more integrated order (the artistic one) with the disorder and the decay that are usually identified with illness. And I am intrigued by the phenomenon of revitalization or the intensification of the will to live sustained by certain people who have suffered and survived a grave disease. In those cases, illness plays the same role as trials and death in ritual initiations: the initiate emerges as if reborn and all-knowing.

It has been said that Sabina has no character, or at most a fragmented one. On the contrary, I believe that she is multifaceted and fills the novelistic space with an energetic presence that emanates from oblique planes of narrative much as the visual planes of a Cubist painting.

Sabina is a composite figure, the embodiment of many characters who split and develop into a multitude of possible characters. All of us are like that, in some way; we live on many levels at once, or at least some of us sustain several personalities at the same time, like Sabina. There is no absence of character in her; on the contrary, perhaps she is excessively rich in possibilities: a woman who contemplates the sea while planning to write a novel; the characters that others see in her; those she imagines surround her; those she dreams she could have been or could still become; and, in addition, her childhood and lifetime acquaintances are incorporated into her being.

Let's digress for a moment to discuss surrealism since you refer to it in your works, and some of Sabina's *structure seems to approximate surrealist linking.*

But *Sabina* is not surrealist automatic writing because there was a deliberate system, an outline for *Sabina.* The associations are free only up to a certain point; free but oriented, guided.

In Sabina, *more so than in* Muerte por agua *or* Celina o los gatos, *the female character-narrator is very important. She even mistreats the male author in the "Labyrinth Room" and refuses to serve as a character in his novel when she realizes he intends to give her a marginal role in a "nonfiction" novel in the style of Truman Capote's* In Cold Blood. *Would you comment on your interest in women authors like Gertrude Stein, Virginia Woolf, Emily Brontë, and the obvious predominance of women in your works?*

That is not deliberate. It must be totally unconscious. Surely since my point of view is that of a woman I customarily turn to or remember other women writers whose sensitivities might approximate my own. I do believe that women may lead different lives than men. I'm not quite sure of this but I suspect there must be some difference between the world views of men and of women. But I don't think I treated the male character of the novelist poorly in *Sabina*.

You called him a nonentity.

But then I deny everything I've said.

Then later you refer to him as a spy.

It's all rather burlesque. I imagined him as a character who wants to write an absolutely objective novel about a true, clear story.

Like In Cold Blood.

Like *In Cold Blood*. So the fact that he's a man is purely accidental. He could have been a woman.

But he wasn't. You know in Rayuela *by Julio Cortázar, the author refers to the "lector hembra" (female reader)—the passive reader who cannot comprehend nor deal with complicated novels.*

That's pure misogyny on his part.

Yes. When I interviewed him, he confessed that it was a foolish move on his part. He recognized it as a purely cultural "machista" influence on him. Now, eleven years after Rayuela, *I see in* Sabina *a vindication of that female reader. For just as Cortázar used "lector hembra" subconsciously, you, without realizing it, didn't allow the male author, who wants to mirror reality rather than invent it creatively, to get the upper hand. Only the woman writer prevails.*

Perhaps so, unconsciously.

In Sabina, *you capture the reader's interest in many ways. Perhaps most traditionally, you create suspense with the possible suicide of the protagonist. To what extent do your obsessions with shipwrecks and drownings, insanity, and suicide feed on one another?*

The nuclear anecdote that is never really told would be about a woman who ends up committing suicide or being assassinated.

88

Is it true, as stated in the novel, that such a suicide notice appeared in the newspaper about a woman in Acapulco?

Yes, I took the announcement verbatim from the newspaper. It was never clear as to whether or not it was suicide or murder. But it was a man, not a woman who died. When I was about to complete *Sabina,* in the last days, I saw the newspaper article. It seemed very curious that while I was writing the novel, all of a sudden I ran across that very news item about a man who died in Acapulco under similar circumstances. From the start I had already chosen that ending.

As one advances in the reading of Sabina, *certain relationships and coincidences are clarified and the narrator begins to frantically summarize possible interpretations. For example, in one passage you reiterate the words "you said" as if in a litany. Would you comment on the need to accumulate and thus review, to offer certain keys to the readers so they might understand the novel better? Because, in fact, those review lists bring about the opposite result. The readers have become so accustomed to denial or negation of previously proferred positive information that they no longer have confidence in the gift of clues.*

That is precisely the objective: to plant clues in order to disconcert the readers even more; to tell them there is no single possible reading but rather many, many probable readings and that each reader must seek a unique reading, not a passive one, as Cortázar would say. The reader must be active all the time, as active as the writer or another character in the book. Thus all apparent clues are false because the book is simply a series of suggestions or stimuli I propose to all readers so they can each construct a personal book.

Sabina *plays with, defies, and makes fun of many contemporary literary movements: the French "new novel," the psychological novel, the Latin American epic novel, the best-seller. But at the same time,* Sabina *shares certain traits with them. As a result,* Sabina *pokes fun at itself for its incapacity to be totally different and original.*

Yes. *Sabina* proposes irony to deal with certain schools like the "boom" novel in Latin America. Every book is an absolutely authentic phenomenon only in so far as it responds to the author's needs. We all write within a period with antecedents, with contemporaries; but every book must be understood on the basis of its own motives, within its own space. Yes, I even poke fun at my own incapacity to achieve all I wanted to in that book.

You say that on the first page of Sabina*: "I cannot have confidence in words."*

I don't believe that nowadays we can be overly confident in the power of words.

But on the same page you contradict yourself and say, as you do in Función de la novela, *that words are our only salvation.*

Exactly. For me they are the only possible hope; nevertheless, I know, lucidly, rationally, that they are a precarious life preserver. But they are all I have within reach. The book always exhibits that double, ambiguous, ambivalent nature, just like our existence. We know we are mortal, that we are going to die, and, yet, at the same time, we have this tremendous need to survive, to leave behind something articulate.

I'd like to hear about the various leitmotifs that appear frequently in Sabina*: photographs, spiral shells, paintings, cats, the color yellow, the sea, roses.*

In *Sabina*, all those motifs that have pursued me in my fiction seem to coalesce. Almost all of these symbols possess an ambivalent or contradictory nature: at once they are signs of heaven and hell. During different periods, for example, the cat has been angelical or demoniac. Life was generated in the sea; but the sea's expanse is abysmal. It is death, darkness, night, adventure, refuge, and shipwrecks. The rose embodies perfect beauty but is short-lived. It hangs in the balance between beauty and death, one of my obsessions.

As I intimated earlier, to me the main theme of Sabina *lies in your challenge to time, to forgetfulness, and ultimately to death. In order to achieve this, you have erected a contradictory system in the novel, whereby a physically immobile woman reaches out to the sea with such dynamism and vitality of thought that her creative mind fills the void with energy without contributing to the linear passage of historic time. How did you finally create the willful duel between the author and her protagonist when the latter decides to break with the synchronic time of*

90

the novel by leaping to her death in the sea but the former, her creator, prevents the character from expiring on the rocks below, compelling her instead to groan and sigh with the memory of her infinitely open view of the sea?

I have the author state that she has created Sabina; therefore, the character depends on the writer for her life and the author chooses to keep her alive as long as the book may have readers. This is only one of the readings; but there is another version in which every character somehow exists with a life wrenched from the author. I peel off a skin every time I write and give it to my characters, who live a borrowed life. So, as not to die altogether, I give pieces of my being to my literary progeny; they keep me alive with every reading. You know, still another version of my book exists, perhaps the most intimate one. I think that the fictitious suicide is my way of conjuring a spell, a kind of exorcism of my own death; through the death of my characters, I avoid death in real life.

I understand that you are presently at work on another novel.

Yes, a book that was originally a story about a couple and an island. The couple would be archetypical and would encompass all the famous couples of literature and history. I can imagine a couple that would be Tristan and Isolde, Romeo and Juliet, Adam and Eve, Solomon and the Shulamite, all at once. This couple's encounters and separations form an impassioned discourse that alternates with a reflexive discourse on utopias. That Western idea of paradise has been imagined by Thomas More and other philosophers and poets. It is a utopia or paradise lost that one tries to recover without ever reaching it. Whenever a couple appears, a utopian island surfaces, the utopia of the imaginary space par excellence where love achieves perfection. At first in my book the island was a geographic place where the characters met or planned to meet, an island where a fair was taking place. But I feel as if the island itself is going to disappear, little by little, to give way to the utopian discourse replete with quotations about islands from other works and authors. Those quotes will appear in the margin of my text. The island will exist solely as an ideal, imaginary place where lovers rendezvous; but they never do meet for although the couple exists, the utopian island takes shape in their fantasy alone. So I will alternate two kinds of discourse in a text I may call a novel, even though it barely resembles one. It will emerge as a sort of philosophical debate between a rational, lucid, reflexive discourse that clashes with the other one trying to express itself as a passionate discourse. This book differs so much from my previous writing that I am very enthusiastic about it.

Does the situation of the female author in Spanish America differ from that of the male author? Does she have the same opportunities to publish her work and circulate it in her own country? Abroad? In translations? The same opportunities to win national or international literary prizes?

I believe that a woman has to be very good, exceptionally capable in all activities in order to be recognized. It is more difficult for her to achieve acceptance than for a man. It is easier for a mediocre man to get ahead than for a brilliant woman. Nevertheless, once she has been acknowledged, all doors open to her. Or almost all. And perhaps women writers encounter fewer obstacles than those women who are engaged in other pursuits. The publishing houses usually don't harbor prejudices. But I do not know if it is valid to generalize. I can only speak about Mexico and, within that context, of my own experience. I have always been able to publish, since I was twenty years old. Besides, I've been the president of the P.E.N. Club, and I am the editor of a journal (*Revista de la Universidad de México*). Several years ago Octavio Paz invited me to be on the editorial board of *Vuelta*. One of my books won the Villaurrutia Prize. I cannot complain. But I can say that such recognition did not come early, but rather much later than other writers—men—of my generation.

Are there certain taboo themes for women writers that would be accepted more easily by society if the author were a man?

Perhaps there are still certain barriers to sensitivity that are difficult to surmount.

In your fiction, do you consciously or subconsciously broach themes that specifically pertain to the Spanish American woman? Are you concerned with woman's socioeconomic role in Spanish America?

I've never thought about novelistic material in geographic terms. I don't write sociological documents but rather try to create literature. And literature occupies an imaginary space, not that of indices or manifestoes.

Recently, have you been able to earn a living exclusively by writing fiction?

Not in the last few years or ever in my entire life. That portion of my writing that has provided me with steady earnings has been my translations; I've translated some thirty-eight books with the exception of literature (history, economics, psychoanalysis, etc.), and I've taught at the university. In addition, I have a husband who has helped a great deal because, in spite of the fact that he also writes (although not exactly fiction), he knows how to do other things.

What are you writing now? Does it sustain your interests expressed in earlier works? Are there new experiments, directions?

I am presently planning a book. Something quite different, I'd say almost a saga. I want to tell the story of a Cuban family from the end of the nineteenth century up to the present. Several generations, several perspectives on life, the play of destinies. Nothing at all like what I've done up to now. I want to return to a narrative that tells a story. I want to construct solid, well-delineated characters. But I've not yet begun to write this book, except for some notes and a few pages of the first chapter.

Presently, what kind of readings interest you most?

This year I've read the *Memoirs of Hadrian* by Marguerite Yourcenar and *The Sleepwalkers* by Herman Broch. But I've had to read a lot of material for the journal, and there's little time for other things. Besides, my husband's life has impinged on my own plans as never before. I've accompanied him during several months on a political campaign, and now I will go to live in a far-off place—some nine hundred kilometers from Mexico City—where he will be governor for six years. All of this demonstrates, in a concrete way, how being a female author is not the same as being a male author. Now I'm reading a bibliography about the development of small rural communities and am making plans to improve the living conditions of women and families in the countryside. So I think my book—the new one—will probably wait a little.

There are many Spanish American writers who do not live or have not lived at some time in their own countries but rather have written from abroad—for political, social, or personal reasons—in voluntary or involuntary exile: Cortázar, García Márquez, Vargas Llosa, Puig, Donoso. Does this situation apply to women writers from Spanish America? Do they feel the need or desire to distance themselves from their social context? Can they do so as easily as male authors?

Everything hinges on one's personal biography. Some Hispanic American women writers always lived abroad, like Gabriela Mistral. Now I am thinking of Luisa Valenzuela, who lives in New York. But I suppose that for a woman emotional ties count a lot and, consequently, they are more lasting. She is doubly rooted because she forms part of a couple and because of the adherence to her own space full of memories that are, perhaps, more difficult to abandon.

Since we met for the interview, have you written other books? Would you describe the importance you attach to your recently published fiction?

I set about splitting hairs in a study on narration, and so *La herencia obstinada* [The Persistent Legacy] was born. I mean to say that I became involved in the most remote manifestations of the need to tell a tale, in oral tradition, to try to verify something of that enigma or mystery that is the desire to verbalize history. I used the model of structural anthropology (Levi-Strauss) and psychoanalysis (Freud) to analyze stories about an indigenous Nahua community in southern Mexico. Nothing like that had been done among us, and the investigation was fascinating, even though my son has reproached me, as if it were sacrilegious for me to have used scientific methods in order to draw back the veil. And, deep down, I believe that he is right, and I feel somewhat embarrassed.

At the time of the interview, El miedo de perder a Eurídice *had not yet been published and so we talked very little about it. Without asking you detailed questions, could you tell me what importance you attribute to* Eurídice *in the light of your earlier novels?*

94

Eurídice is a metaphor for the poetic experience, the act of writing. To talk of desire is to talk of writing and *Eurídice* is, like most of my books, a mirrored space that reflects me (in another dimension) and reflects the book that I am writing. I also think that it brings a certain cycle of my work to a close and that what I write from now on will be completely different.

Do you consider yourself to be part of a literary generation in Mexico or in Hispano America?

I belong to a generation of writers in Mexico born between 1930 and 1935: Juan García Ponce, Salvador Elizondo, and Sergio Pitol belong to this generation. And I believe that something more than age draws us together: respect for the text as a space in its own right, with a logic that does not belong to the world of historic causality.

Have there been specific experiences in your life that have influenced the way you write?

Yes, my mother's death. My own death began to walk by my side eight years ago (when a malignant lesion appeared), and then was left behind until someday when it may return to fall in step again and catch up with me. I don't know why, but I link that fatal experience with writing. Perhaps one writes in order to conjure death.

What do you think about the "boom" of the Latin American novel?

I have no opinion. Too much has been said about that, and there is nothing to add.

Which women writers in Latin America do you feel are most important?

Among women narrators I like the Brazilians: Clarice Lispector (who is no longer living), Lygia Fagundes Telles, and Nélida Piñón. There are splendid female poets: Blanca Varela in Peru and Olga Orozco in Argentina.

I've read your article published in Vuelta *entitled "Does Writing Have a Sex?" Do you believe that there is such a thing as feminine writing, a female voice in literature?*

I think that writing is androgenous. Creativity frees very archaic images and themes of humanity and in those depths the feminine and masculine are interwoven and blurred. Remember Flaubert proclaiming he was Madame Bovary and Emily Brontë saying through Cathy, "I am Heathcliff." That is the magic of words: to reconcile opposites as in the alchemists' retort.

Elvira Orphée

Argentina

I possess the mysticism of a dark remote past.

Clarice Lispector

Elvira Orphée. (Photo José Eduardo Lamarca.)

Born in San Miguel, Tucumán, Argentina, 1930. Earned B.A. in literature, University of Buenos Aires. Studied at Sorbonne, Paris. Traveled to Italy. Married Miguel Ocampo, an artist. Resided eight years in France, three in Italy, one in Spain. Had three daughters. Received honorable mention in literary contest sponsored by Fabril Publishing Company for the novel *Uno,* 1961. Won second prize from Municipality of Buenos Aires for the novel *Aire tan dulce,* 1967. Won first prize from Municipality of Buenos Aires for the novel *En el fondo,* 1969. Received honorable mention in short story contest held by *Imagen,* 1970.

"Personally, I get chills when I read 'John Doe, married, two children.' What do I care if Werner Von Braun has two children or fourteen? They are inconsequential points of reference. A biography about the unreal qualities of a person would be more revealing. One ought to require biographies made of dreams (dreams without Freud's intervention), with erroneous interpretations, with omissions, with all that is tormenting." (Elvira Orphée, in a letter in answer to a request for information about her life, 1978).

Constant physical illness has besieged Elvira Orphée since childhood and has come to influence her narrative. "The very fact that we possess a body," Orphée claims, "mutilates our freedom."[1] Her youth was "filled with goblins" in the subtropical province of Tucumán "where every house harbored a ghost of sickness." A frail body and a defiant will have combined in Orphée with the mystery and phantasmagoria of those early years in a land where the voices of the Incas seemed to emanate from the timeless rocks of the high plateau inhabited by their ancestors, the Coyas. This primordial essence is breathed into Orphée's narrative as she explores her characters' passions for power and love while struggling to transcend the trivialities of life. Such sociopolitical subjects as Peronism and political torture in Argentina are manipulated by a psychological introspection which focuses on perennial questions that eclipse the limited, historical context. Individual characters embody the immortal forces of good and evil and life and death with a feverish lucidity.

The majority of Orphée's creatures are orphans, social outcasts, and humiliated victims suffering from some kind of acute deficiency. They are unloved, ostracized, impotent in the face of their destinies. Searching to vindicate themselves, recover their freedom, and fulfill their needs, they reach moments of hypersensitivity, vertigo, and cruelty. As such, they inspire horror, like the innocent savagery of the demented child in Orphée's short story "Ballena de seda" (The Silken Whale), which takes its rightful place in Spanish American literature alongside "La gallina degollada" (The Decapitated Chicken) by the Uruguayan Horacio Quiroga and "Macario" by the Mexican Juan Rulfo.

Among modern Spanish American writers who have attempted to communicate the terror of political persecution—Miguel Angel Asturias's *El señor presidente (Mr. President)*, Manuel Puig's *El beso de la mujer araña (The Kiss of the Spider Woman)*, Luisa Valenzuela's "El mejor calzado" ("The Best Shod"), Marta Traba's *Conversación al sur* (Conversations Down South), and Julio Cortázar's "Apocalipsis en Solentiname" ("Apocalypse in Solentiname") and "Segunda vez" ("The Second Time Around")—the cruelty of Orphée's torturers in *La última conquista de el Angel* (Angel's Last Conquest) incarnates a unique, grotesquely "mystical" brutality which seeks access to the unknown. Winkel, the leader of the Secret Police, explains: "If I'm a poor bastard who's only heard of Carrara marble and the color of emeralds, it's not fair for me to die without having experienced their splendor. And so I search for it wherever I can, in the mucous membranes of the soul."[2] Contradictory sentiments of dependence and independence, of idealized love and routine conviviality or physical sex, repeatedly define the insufficiency of relationships between women and men. Orphée denies the possibility of perfect love or supreme bliss, and her characters' searches for an absolute always meet with failure. They persist, however, for the more terrifying the experience, the more happiness they think they will achieve by it. Even family life is portrayed by a lack of attention, harsh discipline, and misunderstanding, causing obsessive reactions from family members such as that of the little girl haunted by her mother's ghost in "Pequeña Ning" (Little Ning) until finally the child detaches the transfusion apparatus sustaining her bedridden parent.

Orphée's characters often hallucinate and thus reveal to the reader their intense terror and hatred. Orphée herself opposes all attempts to psychoanalyze these characters and insists on maintaining a certain air of mystery about herself and her fictitious progeny: "I'm like Borges. I believe that psychology is a science of conjecture and, at least for me, of no attraction except for Jung. Freudian psychology bores me; I consider psychologists marvelous thieves, and Freud a person who, more than others, added to the confusion." Orphée's technique gradually exposes her characters in partial glimpses, preferring the first person narrative and shunning the omniscient point of view. As a result, she achieves a mood of immediacy and intimacy, like that of *Aire tan dulce* (How Sweet the Air), in which she intertwines three separate voices in alternating monologues.

Elliptical dialogue, lyrical introspection, telegraphic rhythm, and analogical rather than chronological linking mark Orphée's prose style. External details and descriptions are so scarce that even the colorful scenery of Tucumán or Rioja is filtered through memories, rendering them oneiric evocations. Although colloquialisms and the "lunfardo" jargon are present in her prose, Orphée's language generally preserves its poetic nuance and cadence even in grotesque situations or in deceptively simple passages:

> The days became warmer and October arrived. The water receding from the tile pavement left it shiny, and the rhomboidal design of the mosaic tiles seemed like terse silk. A black and white harlequin's suit. On top, the water caressing it. The people were thirsty when they saw this because it was starting to get hot and that new heat, that aroma of flowers, transformed the most vague longings into thirst.[3]

Orphée's bare, elemental, and intuitive style hints at her predilection for Japanese writers—Ryunosuke Akutagawa, Yukio Mishima, and Osamu Dazai. Although she insists there are few similarities between her prose and theirs, one can perceive that she employs the same aura of scorn, fear, hatred, and love apparent in Akutagawa's short story "Kesa and Morito" and a similar use of multiple perspectives seen in his "In A Grove." The acute humiliation suffered by Goi in "Yam Gruel" also resembles that of Orphée's Félix Gauna. During the last pages of Mishima's final novel in the tetralogy *The Decay of the Angel,* the narrator describes young Toru: "One half of him was in it [this world]. The other was in that realm of indigo. There were consequently no laws and no regulations that governed him. He but pretended that he was bound by laws of this world. Where are there laws regulating an angel?"[4]

One could easily attribute this description to Orphée's Atala in *Aire tan dulce* or to the nameless protagonist-narrator in *En el fondo* (Beyond): two young women whose physical infirmities confer upon them a ductile and mediumistic aura (their own indigo realm) which transforms their perception of time. The inappropriateness of ethical judgment expressed by Mishima's Toru is suggested by Orphée as well in her treatment of the torturer in *La última conquista de el Angel,* that "priest of deformity" whom she infused with a "divine" revenge whose intensity transgresses the tenets of social morality.

For some time now a primitive sense of divinity and a desire for eternity have permeated Orphée's person and work. In 1961, during an interview, she failed to comprehend why divinity had to be considered a superlative value rather than a common trait.[5] In 1977, while conversing with Alicia Dujovne Ortiz, whose fiction she admires, Orphée reiterated, "I do not have any direct contact with religion. I believe, with Murena, that all churches impose a limitation on God. But my divine sense is, perhaps, permanent."[6] And so she imparts to her characters a cosmic splendor, a primitive omnipotence which eschews ethics more completely with each successive work. Orphée creates her own personal mythology to compensate for a life that lacks the prodigious thrill of power and passion, as Atala's grandmother, Fausta, affirms in *Aire tan dulce:* "You don't need a dirty shawl for life to become radiant. The rain's enough. But you don't even need that if you're permeated with words. That's what stories are for when life's not enough."[7]

In his essay "The Cult of Books," Jorge Luis Borges states that Moslems do not consider the Koran to be a mere work of God but rather one of his attributes, like his eternity or his ire.[8] The sacred scriptures, like all cosmogonies, endeavor to salvage the genesis of the world and to save man from oblivion and silence. Elvira Orphée's "scriptures" also attempt to preserve from forgetfulness the words lost in her infancy and in the mythology of her origins in Tucumán. Her fiction is not just "mere work," as Borges might put it, but one of her attributes like "her" eternity or "her" ire. Her female characters often feel themselves torn from the very rock of the natal mountain, and so does Orphée: "I've always had that sensation, even as a very young child. It has nothing at all to do with Catholic mythology . . . it comes from another dimension, something demoniacal or extraplanetary that animated the stone."

Buenos Aires, Argentina   *17 July 1978*

Do you consider yourself part of a particular literary generation in Argentina?
No.

Do you feel any sort of kinship with other Argentinian writers today?
No.

How and when did you begin to write fiction?
Is that important?

It would be interesting to know.
When I was eleven years old, my life was quite empty, except for ghosts. It was replete with them, for I lived in a province which is much more uninhabited, or at least as desolate as the pampa where you have to create your own mythology. Mine was about the mountains rather than the pampa. But a provincial city is so limited; it possesses so little life or even nighttime light, a terrible, failing light that lends itself to the appearance of ghosts. I've even asked women of my age, "When you lived in Tucumán, weren't there ghosts in every house?" They told me "No." Well, for me, a specter not only lived in every home but also signified illness at times. For example, you couldn't walk in front of a certain bakery because the owner's fingers were chopped off. They said it was leprosy. So everything was imbued with mystery, diseases, apparitions, guilt from afar. Life was filled with imaginative substance but not with events; nothing happened there unless you made it happen. That's how I came to write some foolish verses when I was in school:

One night, a beautiful night,
I beheld your lovely face,
That night, star-filled night,
My love for you began.

When a nun discovered them, a great scandal ensued.

Have your experiences in Tucumán, Europe, and Buenos Aires influenced your writing?

As I mentioned, in Tucumán, the heat, the fear of everything, illness, ghosts. Tucumán marked me because it made me ill, physically ill. I evidently had little resistance to digestive infections and had them all: parasites, amoeba, year after year after year. I began to have intestinal problems as an infant, and they have continued all my life. For me, the experiences of Tucumán and illness represent a great sense of loss. Had I been born in Paris, I would not have yearned for Paris. But I was born in a province full of malaria, poverty, mosquitoes, and lepers, so I longed for Paris. The deficiency made me reach Paris. For a long time I also considered my poor health to be a curse until, suddenly, I discovered that it made me what I am.

In your fiction, illness often appears as both a punishment and a gift: it castigates man for having desired the impossible and it rewards him by forcing him to fix his attention on an insuperable center, thus allowing him to forget his surroundings and to overcome obstacles.

To my way of thinking, physical pain has nothing at all to do with mental or spiritual anguish. In times of extreme crises, I, for one, am radiantly healthy. By the same token, most of Freud's concepts are as ridiculous as those dealing with women; it is not surprising that his theories barely interest me. My characters suffer physically or spiritually, but the latter does not provoke a case of angina.

And the influence of Buenos Aires on your fiction?

At first Buenos Aires seemed hostile, frigid. I don't know how to write novels about the big city; besides, those I've read all seem identical, except those about United States cities. The supernatural dimension in our province is comparable to the demented atmosphere of a city like New York.

I'm glad you've mentioned the atmosphere in Tucumán, because I'm constantly impressed by the atmosphere you create in your fiction by describing places and thoughts. The scant action that transpires occurs in the characters' minds as reactions to the minimal events that surround them and not to any grandiose occurrence.

Let me read you something pertinent to your question in which I was making a distinction between feminine and masculine literature: "First, among men, there is an attitude of scorn and condemnation toward the opposite sex, while among women a very natural attitude prevails with few exceptions. Second difference: a Religion of Power in man as a center, as a sun. There is no equivalent in feminine literature; the narcissistic adoration by women doesn't emerge. Women writers are not priests who officiate at their own altars the way men like D. H. Lawrence do. Last, on a more transcendental level, there is a third difference between a masculine literature of action and a feminine literature of penetration that might seem more static but really is not."

Are there any literary antecedents or experiences you feel have influenced your creative work?

When I read certain Japanese authors, I feel they are my brothers. There is no resemblance, but I would like to write the way they do for they fascinate me.

Do you feel a spiritual kinship?

My soul would like to be like theirs, but it falls short. I can understand Rilke, for example, to whom I am attracted; I can penetrate his modus operandi but I cannot comprehend the Japanese. In Rilke everything is admirable and lucid. I admire him, but I don't sense that he is an odd fellow; those others are. It is their extraplanetary strangeness that seduces me.

I see certain constants in your fiction ever since Dos veranos *(Two Summers). They seem to be fundamental to your work. For example, there is always a character whose inferiority complex makes him feel ridiculed and humiliated to the extent that he is compelled to vent his wrath on his fellow man, almost as if he had a physical need to free himself of a great weight. Thus, envy becomes revenge. These characters recognize and despise this same weakness in others, the failing of a helpless being who must kill and wound to defend the affront to his existence. For example, we have Sixto Riera's first words in* Dos veranos*: "since the dawn of time, I am furious." Or Félix Gauna, who in* Aire tan dulce *despises his father and friends, the whores, Estrellita's father. Incapable of facing those who humiliate him, he seeks a secret revenge and aspires to be the most wicked of all men. Or, in* La última conquista de el Angel, *the narrator challenges life itself for knowing too much when he knows so little. And so he demands to experience the unknown by torturing others. Would you comment on this characteristic sense of inferiority, which manifests itself in evil acts against fellow men?*

These are quite different cases. For example, Sixto Riera is an abandoned child who doesn't know his mother or father. Destiny has marked him, as illness has sealed Atala's fate. Her rebellion is lyrical; she must strike out because she has been harmed. Sixto feels humiliated and wishes he were someone else, someone rich and respected. Finally, his destiny calls. He was marked to be an assassin, but an assassin who doesn't even kill but instead mutilates the face of a dead man. He doesn't seek revenge on the weak; he doesn't bring his wrath to bear upon his fellow man; he's really killing his own destiny, his fate, or, if you wish, God. But, on the other hand, Félix Gauna is simply a petit bourgeois who hates and despises mankind. He is not marked by fate like Sixto, for whom there is no future. Gauna unleashes his anger on the weak and finally ends up envisioning his future mediocrity with a certain resignaation. As for the torturer, he could be no more than a torturer, and he knew well that it was an abominable choice. So it became a matter of vindicating himself by glorifying his role. He began as a patriot, sui generis, besides being a fanatic. Full of admiration and respect for his boss, he took his job as a priesthood. He doesn't seek revenge for personal reasons but rather punishes the traitor; the torturer acts like a priest exorcising a devil.

Another constant in your fiction is an omnipresent disgust that adolescents feel when faced with sexuality, their deception before love. They seem to experience a physical as well as an emotional malaise, a consciousness of mortality, pain, and cruelty. Such is the case of Sixto Riera in Dos veranos, *Atala in* Aire tan dulce, *the narrator in* En el fondo, *and the child in "Los aprendices aprenderán" (Apprentices Will Learn). Love is either an ideal or a hope, and sexuality sickens the characters.*

Love seems impossible for the men and women you create. Sexual violence and perversity or a lack of communication resulting in boring routine appear to prevail. How do you perceive love between men and women?

I conceive it to be absolutely the opposite of the way it is portrayed in my fiction. There, it is unattainable love; precisely, it is love which is not love. It is a lack, a misguided liaison, all that is vulgar.

In Aire tan dulce, *Mimaya and Atala try to achieve eternity by means of love but fail. Wasn't that inevitable?*
To fail?

Yes.
Both believed in pursuing an absolute and evidently the search for an absolute ends in failure.

And must love always be an absolute?
Yes, or else it is not worthwhile.

But if love is conceived as an ideal, as perfect, then it cannot exist.
No. Evidently it must not exist.

Freedom and the lack thereof pervade your fiction. Does free will exist for your characters? Do they achieve liberation only through death, insanity, or at the expense of their fellow men? How do you conceive of freedom?

I would say that the desire for freedom is presented in my books, not freedom itself. Liberty is utopian. No one has ever achieved it. The very fact that we possess a body mutilates our freedom. How can I define something that may exist perhaps in other planetary spheres? I think Lala in *Dos veranos* explains that freedom is nothing more than the suppression of everyday triviality. Do you think it is the ability to shout, "Long live so-and-so"? Is it really the freedom to put food in your mouth, killing yourself at work? The only freedom for us is resignation; we are free to resign ourselves to our destiny. We are free to elect fatality, nothing more. Truly, there is no liberty.

In your fiction a lyrical atmosphere prevails, one that often incorporates phantasmagoric tendencies, dangerous or infernal elements, and a cos-

mic or prehistoric dimension. Your characters yearn to partake of that ambience, to become one with nature, the rain, sun, and moon like Atala in Aire tan dulce. *The narrator in* En el fondo *seeks refuge in a dream-time, whereas the girl in "El cuco de la chica" (The Girl's Boogie Man) imagines herself a vengeful god. How do you explain this mythical bent and the longing for lost eternity, for a timeless space prior to good and evil in which a child named Elvira plays the almighty one arranging the destiny of others?*

I have always had the sensation of having been wrenched from the rock, from the mountain. Since early childhood, I had felt myself emerge, flying forth from the red rock of the hills, as if I had inhabited them. I believe in my Inca ancestors who lived in the high plains. The Inca empire extended as far as Tucumán. I went to Lima once in search of my Indian past. Lima seemed to have the same dark luminosity as Tucumán, a dark sun. The houses in Cuzco are like toothless, gaping mouths with black patios. Something was disturbing, demoniacal; there was no sensation of clarity.

Of eternity?

No, there was no eternity, only a very distant time.

Couldn't it be the difference between a historical impression of time in that city and an ahistorical sensation of atemporality that one finds in nature?

I don't know. I went to Greece once—my other roots, my name is Greek—and the Parthenon at noon left me in awe; that is my ancestry. There stood the temple in which I would have kneeled to pray. But when I say I pulled loose from the rock, I refer also to the people of Cuzco and the high plateau who are still made of stone, chiseled faces of stone. They have no feelings, they have lost their voice in the turmoil of the Conquest. And with the words, they lost their souls. They emerged from the stone into the stone; a stone that walks. I feel a mythology that has nothing at all to do with Catholic mythology. God did not create Adam from clay nor woman from his rib. Some sort of demoniac or extraplanetary thing came from beyond to animate the rock. And suddenly the stone lived and took a human shape that walked away.

109

You seldom describe the external appearance of your characters or even their surroundings. Instead you choose a psychological approach that focuses on reactions, events, and memories. Why do you prefer an introspective style?

I detest descriptions of physical traits and never understood why one must say, in the detective story, for example, "she was wearing a black hat, a green blouse, and a yellow skirt." I once read a wonderful comment about *The Iliad*. Helen's beauty was never described, but the Trojans understood how she had motivated the war. And so one could surmise her beauty. But introspection is more difficult to imagine even when certain incidents prevail, as is the case with the torturers. Nowhere is it stated that they are good or evil. It may be suggested that they are abominable, and all of a sudden, they exhibit human feelings.

These feelings that verge on insanity, death, terror, fear, panic seem to serve as a means for recovering self-control and power over others. For example, in Dos veranos, *"Sixto wants to win, when he triumphs he experiences a paroxysm of power, preceded by a paroxysm of terror; and only then does he feel a kind of happiness: to rule, to oblige, to dominate, himself and others." Do you believe pain is necessary in order to achieve happiness?*

To survive, yes, pain and sorrow are essential. One has to triumph over oneself. The more horrifying an experience may be, the more happiness one may feel by conquering it.

But, must one suffer and be sad or terrified before meriting happiness?
You can never be happy, but you can feel as if you have conquered your fears.

Perhaps we might turn to some more general questions. Which Latin American authors do you prefer to read nowadays?
This kind of question usually creates enemies. I'll answer it anyway. I like isolated books: *La hermosa vida* [Beautiful Life] by the Argentinian Jorge Capello, in which he succeeds in creating a passionate life from the virtually mundane existence of an aging public servant; a prose volume by the first-rate Argentinian poet Enrique Molina entitled *Una sombra donde sueña Camila O'Gorman* [In the Shadow of Camila O'Gorman's Dream]; the extremely intelligent essays by the

Argentinian H. Murena; *Espiritualidad y literatura* [Spirituality and Literature] by the Venezuelan Juan Liscano because it delimits spiritual terrains which we have come to confuse, moving toward one when we seek another; one of Vicente Leñero's books for its craftsmanship; Carmen Naranjo's for the same reason; the Brazilian Jorge Amado for his sumptuous and Baroque style, for his processions of colorful people winding their way through his novels like happy serpents' tails, and for his having made a city the heroine of his books.

Do you have any favorites among the women writers of Latin America?
Carmen Naranjo. The Argentinian Olga Orozco for the breadth of her poetry. Alexandra Pizarnik, who died more than five years ago, for saying so much in so few words. Jorgelina Loubet for her intelligent, fine essays. In narrative, Sara Gallardo for *El país del humo* [Land of Smoke], in which there is no extraneous verbiage. Alicia Dujovne Ortiz for her discovery of lyricism in the grotesque. And some of Silvina Ocampo's short stories.

Do you believe that female artistic creativity in some ways surpasses that of male authors?
In subtlety, yes. Unless the male author is a poet.

Do you believe in a female voice in literature?
I confess that for some time now I have distinguished masculine literature from feminine by means of the derogatory statements made by male authors about women and the explicit exaltation of strength, largely physical and rarely spiritual. Now I realize that this difference between what is masculine and feminine is so powerful that is reaches far beyond the confines of literature.

Does the situation of the female author in Spanish America differ from that of the male author? Does she have the same opportunities to publish her work and circulate it in her own country? Abroad? In translations? The same opportunities to win national or international literary prizes?

At least in my country there is no difference. A woman has the same opportunities to publish as a man. But, in order for a woman's work to reach foreign countries, it may be necessary for her to die. Male authors are translated much more, as if there were a masculine narrative tradition that valued men's modes of narration more than women's. Or as if the former were understood more, perhaps due to habit. I believe the same is true with respect to international prizes; with national ones we are all in equal competition.

Are there certain taboo themes for women writers that would be accepted more easily by society if the author were a man?

I don't believe so. But if I, personally, had to relate one of those taboo themes, I would tell it differently. For example, I do so in *La última conquista de el Angel,* where torture doesn't extract even one curse word from torturers or victims but rather reaches well beyond the atrocious anecdote about the physical mortification of a human being.

In your fiction, do you consciously or subconsciously broach themes that specifically pertain to the Spanish American woman? Are you concerned with woman's socioeconomic role in Spanish America?

I never start with a socioeconomic assumption. Nor do I arrive at one as a goal. It slowly emerges, if necessary, from what happens to the character. Evidently, in my books, woman is more a theme than man. That was unconscious until this last book, *Las viejas fantasiosas* [The Fanciful Old Ladies]. There it was conscious. Furthermore, I consider it rather capricious when some critic says that women "have tended to offer a complementary universe by relying exclusively on feminine figures." It seems to me rather that we have already heard so much about masculine problems that, once and for all, it does not hurt to have absolute female protagonists. Later on, we'll see. I would not say that I deal with subjects that concern the Hispano-American woman but rather a being from various latitudes.

Recently, have you been able to earn a living exclusively by writing fiction?
No.

What are you writing now? Does it sustain your interests expressed in earlier works? Are there new experiments, directions?

112

I am excited about the essay, because of which I had to get into the history of religions, and I remained with it for who knows how long. Apart from the essay, I am writing a novel. If by experimentation you mean innovations in my writing technique, no. I want to write what I enjoy reading: a well-narrated story.

Presently, what kind of readings interest you most?
The lyrical essay.

There are many Spanish American writers who do not live or have not lived at some time in their own countries but rather have written from abroad—for political, social, or personal reasons—in voluntary or involuntary exile: Cortázar, García Márquez, Vargas Llosa, Puig, Donoso. Does this situation apply to women writers from Spanish America? Do they feel the need or desire to distance themselves from their social context? Can they do so as easily as male authors?

If the female writer belongs to the Communist party, she probably has the options of living wherever she pleases, if that is the sense of the question. If it is not, and you mean to ask me whether a woman author can spiritually leave her surroundings more easily, I do not believe it to be a question that depends on sex but on personality.

Since we met for the interview, have you written other books? Would you describe the importance you attach to your recently published fiction?

Las viejas fantasiosas is a collection of short stories that take place in small towns. Neither fantasy nor pure reality. One critic called them "intrareality," that is, an inner reality that imposes itself upon the one who lives it. Every small village in Latin America knows about these facts and events that enter a realm beyond reality in the imagination of people deprived of external life. That is how they nullify the boredom of an existence where tomorrow is the same as today and succeed in making the monotonous sand clock of time flower with malice, abomination, or enchantment. I consider the book important because I have succeeded in narrating with the simple yet fanciful language of the protagonists and in closing each short story logically, for the most part. Or at least logically for the narrator, so surely the intelligent reader will understand.

Marta Traba

Argentina

What very beautiful music I listen to deep within me.
It is composed of geometric figures intertwining
in the air. It is chamber music. Chamber music
lacks a melody. It is a way of expressing silence.
What I write for you is chamber music.

Clarice Lispector

Marta Traba. (Photo Orlando García Valverde, San José, Costa Rica.)

Born in Buenos Aires, Argentina, 1930. Graduated from National University of Buenos Aires as professor in literature (diplomate), 1950. Married Alberto Zalamea; son Gustavo born, 1951. Studied art with Gulio Carlo Argan in Rome and with Pierre Francastel in Paris, 1951–53. Resided in Bogotá, Colombia, 1954–68. Director of art programs on Columbia National Television, 1954. Professor of art history, University of the Américas, 1954–55. Taught television courses on art history, modern art, and Latin American art on Public Television, 1955–66. Professor at University of the Andes, 1956–66. Founder and director of the magazine *Prisma* (Bogotá), 1957. Son Fernando born, 1959. Founder and director of the Museum of Modern Art (Bogotá), 1963–68. Won Casa de las Américas Prize (Cuba) for the novel *Las ceremonias del verano,* 1966. Director of culture and professor at National University of Colombia, 1966–67. Divorced Alberto Zalamea, 1967. Awarded Guggenheim Fellowship, 1968. Resided in Montevideo, Uruguay; married Angel Rama, 1969. Resided in Puerto Rico, 1970–72. Professor at University of Puerto Rico, Río Piedras, 1970–71. Traveled to Chile during week of Allende's fall to visit son and daughter-in-law, 1973. Resided in Caracas, Venezuela, 1973–79. Professor of Latin American art at Caracas Teacher's College, 1977. Research professor at Institute of Art at Central University of Caracas, 1977–79. Resided in Barcelona, Spain, 1979. Resided in Washington, D.C., 1979–82. Lectured at Harvard, University of Massachusetts, Oberlin College, University of Maryland, and Middlebury College, 1979–80. Visiting professor at school of art at Princeton University; operated on for cancer, 1980. Moved to Paris after being denied permanent residence in the United States for unspecified reasons, 1982. Died in a plane crash near Madrid, Spain, 1983.

Marta Traba's fiction represents an undeniable concern about the problems of city life in the ghetto, about the repression of human rights caused by civil strife, and about the effects of both on individuals living in modern Spanish American societies. Traba's talents excel in the sympathetic treatment of individuals mired in the collective web of burgeoning dehumanization and in the unique development of supportive female characters persevering under the pressures of sweeping social and political injustices.

In her first, prize-winning novel, *Las ceremonias del verano* (Summer Rites), Traba introduced the oppressive cityscape composed of housing projects, modeled after the southside of Buenos Aires of her adolescent years. It dominates the pages of one of her most valuable works, her only collection of short stories, *Pasó así* (So It Was). A collection of sixteen brief narratives linked by a common setting in a Bogotá ghetto and by recurrent characters, this volume is a unique representation of the dilemma of identity in the uniformly built metropolitan neighborhoods all over Latin America. Traba relates how these housing projects, originally conceived as a new type of planned community lodging for the lower middle class, have become decrepit. In those projects left unfinished, half-completed buildings begin to rot; a garbage dump is started on land reserved for a plaza; a whorehouse emerges in place of a child care center. The neighborhood becomes shrouded in an all-pervasive atmosphere of homogeneity.

The characters who live in this environment are equally gray, trapped in the hopeless tedium, and resigned to their sad destinies. The ghetto offers them the same sense of security as a prison, according to Traba, an opaque, neutral limbo where happiness and tragedy are banned for their radical natures. Bored, the characters interfere in each other's lives, a neighborhood pastime, engaging in petty intrigues and spying on one another. A very few try meekly to escape the crushing repetition of vacant lots, treeless sidewalks, and ashen buildings. However, their schemes are usually frustrated by commercial or political intervention, hypocrisy, the lack of motivation, or vandalism on the part of the other ghetto inhabitants: when the mayor delivers a truckload of saplings to commemorate the housing project's sixth anniversary, the children decimate them; a young woman's efforts to paint her apartment door and plant a sapling and geraniums in the front of her house to differentiate her hovel from the others meets with defeat when her neighbor implacably mimics her every move; a father and son companionably construct a tower whose one window faces a few trees on the vacant lots that border the project until their neighbors report their activity to the authorities, who force the two to remove, by ordinance, the tower that has destroyed the unified symmetry of the housing development. At times, only death and insanity provide a true means of escape from the barren planned community.

In the best stories of *Pasó así,* Traba builds situations on an imaginative and ironic turn of events or on a few colorful characters who emerge from the shadows of the ghetto. For example, Iván las Cruces and his family are ceremoniously endowed with an apartment in the project as a benevolent gesture by the authorities to those whose lives have been plagued by hunger and misery. Nevertheless, Iván's tragedies persist. It is not long afterwards that the factory doctor informs him that he has a fatal illness. Only then, ironically during Iván's last, salary-compensated days, do he and his family begin to find happiness by busily painting their apartment pure white in an attempt to illuminate and purify a small space in the rubbish and decay that surround their ghetto home. The prospect of imminent death as a release becomes an antidote to the tedium of the community, as does the appearance of a few unusual female characters in some of the stories: the "immortal" grandmother who, raffled off by her family and won by a prostitute, takes her place as the beatific spectator-resident at the whorehouse in the volume's title story, "Pasó así," and Nimia Sánchez, who is remembered only for the exotic giraffes and nude figures embroidered on her velvet pillows, one of which ultimately drives the neighborhood priest insane. In these unusual portraits, Traba depicts a few isolated individuals living in the dehumanized collective communities as the only humane inhabitants: "Had some human being been present, he would have felt wounded. But there were only people."[1]

More than a decade later, Traba published a powerful novel about two women, Irene and Dolores, against a backdrop of historical and political repression in *Conversación al sur* (Conversations Down South). Statements similar to those in *Pasó así* appear in the book, marking an intensification in her concerns for mankind's lack of tolerance and compassion. In this work about torture, disappearance, terror, and anguish caused by civil strife, she asks, "Has pity for fellow man been lost? Because if so, it's as if an entire society had stooped to inhumanity."[2]

A phantasmal Montevideo is the immediate setting: the first part of the novel takes place at Irene's house at the beach and the second half on a bus at night between Irene's home and Dolores's parents' apartment. However, their conversations and numerous flashbacks transport the reader to all the capital cities—Montevideo, Santiago, and Buenos Aires—of South America's Southern Cone countries, as referred to in the book's title. The flashbacks illuminate the tumultuous years of revolutionary and counterrevolutionary activity and the rise and fall of the Allende regime. After five years apart, the two women unearth memories: "We're not conversing, we're disinterring!"[3]

Dolores, a twenty-eight-year-old Uruguayan writer and political activist, arrested by the police when pregnant and tortured until she aborted and suffered organ failure, attempts to submerge herself in routine to forget a past that often persists in nightmares. Irene, an Argentinian actress in her forties, had been accidentally drawn into contact with young revolutionaries through acquaintances and family rather than by political conviction. Their conversations evoke other dialogues sustained by them with other women. Dolores had traveled with the Argentinian Victoria, the daughter of Irene's old friend Elena, for a few days on a mission to Patagonia. Their opposition to their countries' regimes cemented their friendship. Irene had accompanied Elena to May Square in Buenos Aires to protest, with other women, the disappearance of their loved ones, among them Victoria.

During these shared experiences and conversations, the women reveal the physical and psychological ravages caused by the political turmoil in the Southern Cone. The differences in their generations and personal commitments to militancy are explored: "What's happening is you were never a real militant and you found yourself stuck reluctantly in the middle of that fight," Dolores tells Irene. "It's happened to a lot of our older people."[4] Dolores continues struggling with memories of friends who have disappeared, of a dead husband delivered to her in a sealed box, and of the terror of being imprisoned again. Irene, on the other hand, waits for news from Santiago of her son and daughter-in-law caught in the Allende upheaval, all the while grappling with her impotence as a silent observer of the constant violation of human rights that is condoned by the majority of a populace devoid of compassion, accustomed to death and repression.

In the nineteenth century, Latin American writers had broached the subjects of civil strife—torture, terrorism, and political imprisonment. The Argentinian Esteban Echeverría, in the middle of the century, depicted the brutal persecution of one political party by another in his brief narrative "El matadero" (The Slaughterhouse); José Martí, the defender of colonial Cuba's independence from Spain in the late nineteenth century, wrote a lyrical and dramatic essay, "El presidio político en Cuba" (The Political Prison in Cuba), from personal experience at the age of eighteen. And in the first half of the twentieth century, the Guatemalan Nobel Prize winner Miguel Angel Asturias dealt with the terrorism of dictatorial regimes in his novel *El señor presidente* (*Mr. President*).

Conversación al sur, therefore, perpetuates a tradition of authors, especially Argentinian ones, committed to exposing the truth about terrorism, political imprisonment and repression. Other recent works in this tradition include Jacobo Timerman's autobiographical account *Preso sin nombre, celda sin número* (*Prisoner without a Name, Cell without a Number*); Manuel Puig's novel *El beso de la mujer araña* (*The Kiss of the Spider Woman*); Julio Cortázar's novel *Libro de Manuel* (*Manuel's Manual*), his comic book *nouvelle, Fantomas contra los vampiros internacionales* (Fantomas Fights the International Vampires), and short stories like "Apocalipsis en Solentiname" ("Apocalypse in Solentiname"); Elvira Orphée's narrative *La última conquista de el Angel* (Angel's Last Conquest); Luisa Valenzuela's novel *Como en la guerra* (*He Who Searches*) and short stories like "El mejor calzado" ("The Best Shod"); and Griselda Gambaro's play *El campo* (*The Camp*).

These more recent works vary considerably in their focus and approach. Traba's *Conversación al sur* structurally resembles Puig's novel. Both are based on a series of conversations, but Puig's novel is limited to the dialogue between two cellmates without the intervention of a narrator. Traba, on the other hand, employs the first person narrations of Irene and Dolores and then alternates with a third, omniscient voice that accompanies each of the women's. This contrapuntal style maintains the multiple perspectives present in Traba's earlier novels and allows the constant retrospection that serves to actualize past horrors while simultaneously relating the incidents at arm's length, in a dispassionate tone. This subtle, stimulating technique provokes reader reactions of both dread and pathos, as in the following passage in which Dolores's words are filtered through Irene's thoughts:

> All of a sudden, she began to classify the torture methods as if she spoke of vegetable species. In other days it would have been an unthinkable conversation. I don't know, for some time now everything has changed. While we smoke a cigarette or have a cup of coffee it's possible to mention how someone's been forced to swallow his feces or drink his urine; everyone remains unperturbed; it wouldn't occur to anyone to begin to howl or to throw himself out the window. These things can occur, Dolores continued, what's important is survival and when that happens to you, you're no longer the same person. Do you see? It's very strange, as if they'd broken you for life and made you immortal. It must be just that, in order for her, thrown face down, nude, kicked until she fainted, in the sixth month of pregnancy, to consider herself among the lucky since she is here, now, talking with me about the misfortune of others.[5]

The sensitive development of a sympathetic and symbiotic relationship between two female characters is a unique contribution to Latin American literature. The women share a sense of persecution and the experience of ostracism: Dolores's old friends are afraid to greet her for fear of reprisals and Irene, returning clandestinely to Buenos Aires on a tour bus from Iguazú Falls, feels like a Jew among fanatic countrymen whose "Argentina *über alles*" mentality alienates her from them.

Certain isolated episodes, such as the Iguazú bus ride and the visit to May Square, highlight Traba's dramatic mastery. When she recounts the May Square demonstration in which hundreds of women gather every Thursday afternoon to protest the disappearance of family and friends—in which the aged, infants, and children raise photographs, list names, and wave white handkerchiefs into the air in a pathetic gesture—before the Pink Palace, the government building and the

Cathedral, Traba vividly captures the defiance of these women and the madness of a populace that collectively turns its back on them, condoning the systematic extermination of their fellow men. Traba likens this historical reality to that of the Nazi annihilation of the Jews while the world turned its head the other way. Irene realized that during this pitifully brave demonstration everyone who usually filled the plaza— vendors, priests, soldiers, police—had abandoned it like rats for the two or three hours that the aggrieved women shouted, "Where are they?" The ironic, critical commentary rings clear: "The system was to ignore them; ignore the existence of the plaza and the crazy women who had a tantrum. Had they reached that degree of refinement? Why not, if they were on the same level as far as torture and disappearances were concerned. A developed country does things well."[6]

Caracas, Venezuela 25 *April 1978*

Shall we begin by talking a little about literary generations?

I belong to none because I've never lived in one single country. Coexisting in a generation of that sort implies going to the same university, frequenting the same cafés, appearing in the same magazines, writing for the same newspapers. That is what creates a certain generational cohesion. I've not lived in one fixed place since I was twenty years old, so I feel perfectly footloose.

Have your moves influenced your writing?

Yes, evidently. I left Argentina because I didn't like it there at all, not at all. I left when I was only twenty years old. I studied there in the university during the very turbulent years of Perón's rise to power. Many conflicts filled university life; we studied very little and agitated politically as much as possible. I wanted to leave the university as soon as I was able to get my degree and dedicate myself to an extra-academic field. Besides, during those adolescent years, thousands of immigrants, Italian immigrants, arrived daily in Buenos Aires. Those were the days of Perón's open arms immigration policy; the Italian immigrant even changed the language of Buenos Aires. It was terrible, a virtual battle to live. And that's no metaphor. Within a very short time, the city grew, tripled in demographic density. There were no public services or means of coping with such a deluge of people. The city was caught unprepared. Life was hard in Buenos Aires during my adolescent years. I remember taking bus No. 60 from my neighborhood to downtown where I used to go to school. I spent hours in that bus, crowded in like someone in a concentration camp. Everything seemed tough, arduous, horrible, conflictive. I liked neither the city nor the people's temperament.

You describe city life in some of your fiction.

Yes. Memories persist as they did for Proust. In the novel *Homérica Latina* [A Latin American Epic], the greatest number of pages is dedicated to Buenos Aires and to the time spent on bus No. 60. Moreover, the characters cannot get off the bus; symbolically it becomes a prison where they spend their life. Then, of course, the neighborhoods of Buenos Aires where I lived are described in *Pasó así*.

They're not descriptions of Bogotá?

No, they're in Buenos Aires. Of course, these same shocking neighborhoods exist in Bogotá and other Latn American cities: uniform, anonymous urban wastelands. The marginal districts in a city are the most populated ones. So you have a similar situation in Bogotá: a totally amorphous area, lacking character, where people fight like mad to retain their individuality in the face of homogeneity. I lived that personal experience in Buenos Aires as a child, and it branded me forever. The urban plight and struggle, the slum's anonymity comprise my literary context.

When did you leave Buenos Aires?

I graduated at twenty and then left for Europe. I never wanted to return. I bought a one-way passage aboard a ship to Rome, a kind of pilgrimage for me. I knew no one there, but I wanted to live in Rome.

The scenes in Los laberintos insolados *(Sunstroke Labyrinths) and in* Las ceremonias del verano *are from Italy?*

Yes, everything. I don't know how authors can write what they have not experienced personally. As for me, I could never write exclusively from imagination without reference to reality. *Las ceremonias* is autobiographical, as are all the other books. I find it difficult to create characters and feel as if I fail in this regard. But I do not know how to evoke an atmosphere. Katherine Mansfield's work has always impressed me, her way of observing details, even those that seem to be unimportant.

Regarding your comment about atmosphere, it seems to me that at times, in both Las ceremonias del verano *and* Los laberintos insolados, *architectural descriptions become animated and, at other times, petrified as if by some hallucinatory beauty. In other descritions, in* Pasó así, *for example, monotony and sameness cast gray shadows of sadness and fatality over the scenes and buildings. The narrator's gaze, in all instances, reveals the soul of the work in the settings, the city, rather than in the characters' relationships with each other, their actions, or dialogues. This all leads to my question concerning your profession as an art critic and whether or not your mastery of such vital evocations has something to do with that profession?*

Yes, that is so, and well put. However, I'm not sure which comes first: my profession as an art critic or my interest in visual perception. But one thing is certain. Man is surrounded by beauty and horror, and they impinge permanently on his attitudes. He is surrounded by the world, in a Renaissance sense, and more intimately by his own room in which he has no choice but to deal with himself. The street and the room are two settings in which I, more than my characters, move. Do you understand? That is why it is difficult to create characters. It would be as if I were taking leave of myself—to whom I'm tied—not because of vanity or egotism but because of the fatality of being what I am. I think that is a feminine perspective. Curiously enough, although I am no feminist, I believe in feminine literature, in a tender regard for detail that is not perceived by men. I find this tendency in Carson McCullers, Sylvia Plath, Katherine Mansfield, but not in the very intelligent but practically masculine Virginia Woolf, who is capable of a writing that is strong and solid rather than riddled and devoured by details, by the joy of minute descriptions. I believe that women perceive reality more keenly than men; they grasp what lies in between the cracks. Man encompasses more and possesses a well-ordered, organized intellect. But women behold what is interstitial; it is a very specific, tender, feminine view, and one that I share.

But a woman's vision of detail is not always tender. For instance, even in your narrative an element of horror prevails.

Yes, of course, but that horror is covered or protected by the feminine perception. For example, let's take Clarice Lispector's view, a terrifying description of cold reality that masks another reality beyond the apparent one.

In her works, concrete detail is many-faceted. She animates invisible, imperceptible details.

She reaches beyond reality to penetrate another dimension. It is as if reality were transparent, and she passed through it to communicate with the other. In her novel *A paixão segundo G. H.* (Passion according to G. H.), Clarice describes the character observing a cockroach, a completely repugnant theme that doesn't seem at all repulsive because the descriptions of minute details are neither horrible nor disgusting. The precision of her words covers that reality with a fascination for detail. We women have the power to enchant the reader with details.

Why is that so?

Because we live much more intimately within reality. Men parcel out their lives among specific interests. We women coexist as human beings with everything: the rotten, the beautiful, the garbage, the kitchen, children's crap. Thus women have a knack for things, visual or tactile, that men do not.

And what of the French writer of the "new novel" who may be male, perhaps, and yet focuses obsessively on details?

He does so in a cold, mechanical way that has nothing at all to do with the sensual approach I've described. Rather than an intellecutal game, I am referring to a sensual cascade.

You know, the best passages in your narrative fit that description. For example, you take an object, like a window framing the sky or a van or an airplane, and develop it into an expressionistic flight of imagination that soars beyond the concrete reality of the object. For example, in Las ceremonias del verano, *a woman observes a minimal expanse of skin and from its warmth the sensual description expands to include a forest, a fire, a beach. But, let's return to Rome.*

After Rome, I lived in Paris for a year and was married there. I didn't want my child to be born in Paris because we were so very poor and life was so difficult there for a student, so I returned to Buenos Aires where my first son was born. We stayed for less than two years and then returned to Rome for two years, more or less, before leaving for Colombia. I have spent most of my adult life in Colombia, fifteen years, though I have traveled often. And it was there I began to work as a professional art critic in an atmosphere where eulogies abound instead of art criticism. I never wrote fiction but was an art critic at the university, on television, and in the media wherever cultural programs are initiated. I wrote *Las ceremonias* in Bogotá, curiously enough. I had an enormous amount of work and very little free time. But Antonia Palacios urged me to write fiction. I never dared to try; I was afraid. As an art critic I had begun to develop an organized methodology appropriate to that type of work and had completely abandoned the idea of fiction. But when I wrote *Los cuatro monstruos cardinales* (The Four Cardinal Monsters), I realized that I had already freed the demons in that middle road between criticism and fiction. When Antonia Palacios read it, she called me to say that I should write my first novel even though it might turn out worthless, that I had to wrench it from myself, no matter how. I wrote *Las ceremonias* during a month's time.

Did you then revise it?

Not at all; not a word. When it was finished, Antonia advised me to send it to Cuba to *Casa de las Américas* which, at the time, had the most serious literary competitions in Latin America. Besides, the judges were extraordinary—Carpentier, García Ponce, Manuel Rojas. I never thought I'd win.

How did you hit upon the profession of being an art critic?

I began by studying art in Argentina. Paintings offered me a kind of libidinous pleasure. I specialized in art, and later in France I studied with Pierre Francastel. So you see when I began to write novels, I found myself in a strange position: I was very well known as an art critic in Latin America, but as a novelist I was in square one. Those who knew me as an art critic gave me no credit as a novelist. The Americans have recognized me more as a novelist. You know, Latin American art is scarcely known in the United States. Your marvelous universities have everything but hardly a book or slide on Latin American art.

Not even Mexican art?

A little. But apart from Mexico, Latin America does not exist. So when I came to the states no one invited me to talk about the "nonexistent" plastic arts in Latin America. Instead, they asked me to comment on my novels. My novels were received well in Spain, also. However, in Colombia no one was even aware that I had written them.

But you began your profession as an art critic in Bogotá and organized the museum there?

Yes. And Colombia has influenced me a great deal. My world view was established there, not in Argentina. I feel close to Colombian reality: the poverty, the hard life there, the sincerity of collective society.

In La jugada del sexto día *(And on the Sixth Day), which takes place in Bogotá, you seem to deal with two major groups of characters and settings: the lower class neighborhoods and their inhabitants and the more sophisticated upper middle class and their environment.*

Yes. What's more, my recent novel *Homérica Latina* takes place in all the cities where I've lived. More than a novel, it is a chronicle that functions as a linear text. I've always loved the chronicles written by the Spaniards during the Conquest because they discovered another world and described everything with a great deal of importance. There are few hierarchies. In *Homérica Latina,* I set out to write a novel as if it were a chronicle because in Latin America, the people perceive things on an even level, without great differentiations. I refer to the lower middle class, not the proletariat.

But the class of people which appears in the short stories of Pasó así *is not the same as the one in the novel* La jugada del sexto día.

Of course not. The novel deals critically with Bogotá's upper class. I lived among those people because of my marriage. In *Homérica Latina,* only one day is described in Bogotá, the day the Pope visits the city, a day when everything is transformed by his arrival. The action occurs on two levels. There is the roundup of thousands upon thousands of beggar boys who are locked away so the Pope won't see them and so that the city looks clean. That massive roundup constitutes one level and the other occurs in an apartment situated, symbolically, on the top floor of a building, where a group of sophisticated, refined intellectuals converse, shut away from a city besieged by the police.

Although you seem to concentrate on two different social classes, characters from both confront similar problems: lack of communication, relationships based on superiority and inferiority, hostility, and cruelty, and victimization.

Perhaps it is so because I believe that those terrible situations are realistic for everyone. They are difficult and complex, full of pain and

129

sadness that one must conquer to find happiness. It is not a pessimistic vision, for despite such a reality there is hope.

But in your short stories, the only characters who truly escape from the tenements are Iván, who dies, or the young woman who leaves one hell for another. Those who try to escape, who have dreams, cannot free themselves from their condition.

How curious.

You even intimate that those who live in that neighborhood feel more secure there in their namelessness.

I'm not a negative person in my private or public life, and yet whatever I write comes out sadder each time. The episodes in *Homérica Latina* are extremely touching and pitiful. Only at the end does hope appear to two young people on a bus. They've been tortured and are broken, but they're happy. All of a sudden the young man realizes how strange it is that she has no fingernails, only black and blue fingers where they pulled the nails out. I don't know why my writing inevitably describes relentless sorrow. Perhaps because it is the true nature of life. Happiness is transitory in the realm where man moves, his is a tragic, terrible existence.

Did you move here to Caracas from Bogotá?

I got divorced in Bogotá. In 1966 I was at the university and, I believe, Rockefeller came to Bogotá and was brought to the university as an act of provocation by the president of the republic. The students reacted strongly, and the army entered the university grounds for the first time and turned it upside down. They smashed everything, wrecked labs, and dragged away students to lock them up (they released them later because they ran out of room). In any case, the university became a battleground besieged by tanks. The next day, the press asked my opinion about a sculpture that was to be erected, and I answered that I could not talk about sculptures or anything at a moment when I only wanted the people to walk through the university campus to see what those vandals had done to it. Ten minutes after the papers came out, the chief of the Colombian Armed Forces told the president to throw me out of the country. And he did; he gave me twenty-four hours to leave with my children. I was still an Argentine citizen so they were about to expel me with my two sons. Within those twenty-four hours, the entire country came to my defense. It was unbelievable. That's why I harbor such love and gratitude for Colombia. Thousands upon thousands of letters, telegrams, telephone calls, meetings. The government felt overwhelmed by a public opinion that had never been so strong or unified; suddenly the people declared, "No, you are not going to exile her from this country." So eight lawyers began to work on my case, and the government delayed its decision for a couple of weeks until the president called me to say that he did not know that I had two Colombian sons. Of course, he knew very well, but he had to find an honorable way out. And so for that reason he would pardon me and let me stay in Colombia; but I had to leave the university. I did; I lost everything, but I remained in Colombia. Around then I met Angel [Rama], and after that catastrophe in the university I began to receive letters from various museum directors in the United States asking me to present myself for a Guggenheim; they would support me. I did that, and I won a fellowship. And so I began to travel throughout Latin America. I left Colombia and went to Uruguay where Angel and I decided to live together. We were married later and went to Puerto Rico. It was our longest trip. We were there for two years before returning to Uruguay. But life was very arduous in Uruguay, one couldn't work at the university. So we moved to Caracas and have been here for five years now.

Did you find it hard to concentrate on fiction writing while you worked on art criticism?
No, fiction is my greatest joy. I feel much happier writing fiction. But after the first few books, I began to think that something was amiss, too easy, perhaps mediocre, that I ought to work in a more serious fashion and not let myself be carried away by a sort of spontaneity. So for the first time, I started to work more carefully. Angel influenced me and taught me to correct drafts. It may seem absurd, but with the first four books, I scarcely revised a word. You can't continue that way.

But now that you're planning to leave for Spain, will you continue to write fiction there?
Yes, I have another way of writing since *Homérica Latina*. I began to write that book in Puerto Rico as a series of anecdotes that might form

an unstructured chronicle based solely on a juxtaposition of discrete events. The material grew and coalesced from 1972 until 1976 in Puerto Rico. I consider it to be my first serious book.

We've not discussed literary influences on your fiction.

English literature fascinates me. English and North American—Henry James and Sylvia Plath, for instance. To me no one surpasses Carson McCullers. And as far as women authors in Latin America are concerned, Clarice Lispector is an impressive figure. In fact, women authors interest me more than the men. Djuna Barnes is incredible and so is Erica Jong. They are extraordinary story tellers, superior to male authors.

You wrote novels first, not short stories. And yet in those first novels there is a notable fragmentation of situation and structure which forms isolated episodes which seem like long short stories. On the other hand, in your book of short stories, Pasó así, *the reiteration of certain constants—the neighborhood, the characters—unifies the stories as if the totality were a fragmented novel. What, precisely, is your attitude toward genre differentiation? Do you use genre for specific ends?*

No. Honestly I feel that I am quite confused with respect to genre and its limits. Thematic necessity guides me to reiterate, as you have aptly perceived, a kind of unique setting. Although I'm as capable of planning as Vargas Llosa, for example, the episodes take over, the situations dominate more than the plot line. One day we spoke for a long time with Julio Cortázar about this, the way that Gabo [Gabriel García Márquez] develops a plot of exceptional situations. I cannot do that. My world consists of everyday happenings. Trivialities seem to me transfused with splendor. I feel that we Latin Americans represent an anthropological point of view, outlined by Lévi-Strauss or Mircea Eliade, an essential rather than rational outlook, or rather one that straddles the primordial and the rational. That primitive force does not have to be expressed in an epic form; nevertheless, myth overcomes the contradictions in our societies. The irrationality of myths may be depicted by fragmentaton, which I consider to be a permanent element on our continents. That's why I admire Julio so. Apart from the experimental nature of his extraordinary *Rayuela,* he set the tone for a certain type of work that could be carried out with variations, and that was totally different from the experimental novel in France.

132

To me the most accomplished passages in your narrative style are usually fragmentary and analogic; they burst upon the page and function through a free association that vitalizes the prose.

Certain passages impose themselves on me in a fragmented form, but as I begin to work them into the prose they become a total reality to me. The passages intensify and are no longer subordinated to the action. They take over completely.

And also capture the reader's attention.

Angel says my prose creates an impression of breathlessness. I don't have a critical distance to be able to tell whether or not these descriptive eruptions distract the reader. You see, the reader should involve himself as intensely in the narrative as I did in the writing. Although the narrative may be fragmentary, there must be a thread of continuity, and I don't know if those lyrical or pictorial passages disrupt that continuity.

On the contrary, I feel that they are examples of your finest narrative style. But Angel is right. Those passages are so breathtaking that one is shocked upon returning to the principal narrative action. Let's turn for a moment to the question of the metamorphosis of reality in your works. You seem to help the characters nullify their unpleasant circumstances by means of their highly attuned senses, or rather with your imaginative flair for the expressionistic descriptions that I mentioned earlier. In one of your books you explain this process: "What is life but a constant succession of images; how could one live, how, without the power to metamorphose reality?" I'd like you to comment on the mutation of reality that you achieve when focusing in detail on a single object that suddenly transforms endlessly, at times grotesquely, in an expressionistic passage which relies heavily on visual and sometimes on olfactory or aural representations.

That's a very precise observation, and one that refers to the sordid, tragic, fatalistic situations about which we spoke before. For salvation lies in the imagination. It was my salvation during a sad childhood, and is so even today. One can always seek a personal haven through the power of imagination, a critical stance before reality and the grotesque. Irony and poetry nourish creativity. The grotesque is tinged with irony that neutralizes terrible situations by using humor. Poetry and irony not only save us from our surroundings but also modify and correct reality. Angel says I'll never be a great author because I refuse to see certain things. For example, I could never watch a film about concentration camps. I go to the movies a lot, but I can't watch certain terrible scenes, cruel ones in the movies nowadays. And Angel tells me I must watch them because I ought to deal with them the way great novelists touch upon such horror.

But horror exists in many shapes. There is the bloody kind, but there is also the terror that you express when dealing with everyday existence.

Yes, it is also horrible. There are perverse people who don't interest me at all. Pornography doesn't either, or the kind of novels Puig is writing now. I don't even trouble myself by reading them. I'm not interested in vulgarity, bestiality, unleashed pornography, man and his animal instincts.

Which Latin American authors do you like?

Rulfo and Onetti are wonderful. Onetti's work is first-rate.

And incredibly gray like your fictitious settings.

Yes. In that sense I feel a kinship with him. I respect many writers who are not necessarily part of the "boom," aside from Cortázar, of course, whose short stories are marvelous. But I feel closer to Onetti and Felisberto Hernández.

Why Felisberto Hernández?

For his tenderness. . . .

I was surprised and puzzled at first to hear you mention Hernández, because I thought only of his fantastic short stories. But now that I reflect, I get the impression that you must be attracted to the atmosphere of hopelessness and fatality in his narrative.

Yes.

A kind of despair that one finds in Rulfo's and Onetti's characters as well.

Absolutely. I feel close to Felisberto. To me, Julio is not a desperate person. Onetti, on the other hand, or Felisberto, would close himself off in a room, and Rulfo would remain terrified, locked behind the door without answering the phone during eight months. That could happen to me.

Corralled.

I feel that could happen to me if it weren't for Angel or my sons.

And what of women authors in Latin America aside from Clarice Lispector?

I have very little in common with them. There are many Argentinian women who write well, but I don't feel close to them.

Do you know Armonía Somers's short stories?

Yes, of course. I feel close to her. I'd forgotten about Armonía, for a moment. You did well to remind me because I respect her work a great deal.

She, too, demonstrates a certain cynical attitude toward love in her fiction. In your novel, La jugada del sexto día, *for example, the characters sense a need to communicate with each other in order to escape solitude, and yet their relationships are either frustrated or short-lived.*

I don't think that is cynical. It is just that you can only understand someone else up to a point; no matter how much you may adore him, certain impassable zones remain untouched. Besides, men and women can never communicate with each other completely because their experiences are so very different. Sometimes it's useless to even talk because understanding one another is futile. Silence and solitude somehow attest to the unattainable absolute relationship between the sexes, to a utopia. All relationships are precarious.

Yet your characters, in their silence and solitude, often seem to value objects more than human beings. In Las ceremonias del verano *you allude to "the metaphysical silence of objects." However, death or social situations often intervene to bring the spellbound observer back to reality.*

Exactly. Looking out from my window produces tranquility in me. My eye fixes like an anchor on a tree in the breeze. That is absolute perfection. An object can achieve that perfection, and I realize that is a fiction. But I desire such a fiction, to remain contemplating a beautiful object, totally gratified by it, by that perfect lie. And yet that lie must be destroyed; the illusion of eternal perfection is shattered by death. I myself try to destroy such objects or characters or situations when I feel they promote such deceptions. Therefore, my narratives exist on the fringes of contemplated perfection, anchored to an object, threatened by destruction and death.

This link between the object and death in certain scenes of La jugada del sexto día, *for example, reminds me of paintings by Giorgio de Chirico.*

All of my work is nourished by painting, by visual imagery like that of Piranesi or Delvaux. My characters almost always exist among cultural objects that represent a perfect fiction or a catalyst for achieving zones of perfection. But when those same characters leave those ideal realms for various reasons and return to reality, other cultural objects captivate them again. Man lives immersed in culture, and it is simply a question of how he uses it or how it saves or destroys him.

Sometimes sounds also seem more important than words in your narrative. Train whistles, sirens, murmurs. Besides, words often destroy relationships between your characters.

Words are trivial. A man asks if the shower is warm or why dinner isn't ready. Life together becomes reduced to how much potatoes cost. That's why I feel silence to be more eloquent and important.

Is that why you insist so on visual perceptions?

Yes, of course. And sounds are very disturbing to me, city noises, for example. On a balcony or from a window in the city by night, the sounds are absolutely bloodcurdling. Someone shouts from afar as if from another world. Sounds surround us all the time. Right now, listen to the cicadas.

You spoke before about the novels you are writing now.

Yes, *Homérica Latina* is the climax of an externally oriented vision of my surroundings and of the city. *La casa sin fin* (The Endless House), a short novel I've just finished, is the beginning of another stage in which all external supports and alibis are deliberately abandoned—objects, beauty, cultural salvation. Man confronts himself, closed off and alone.

Why do you have this sensation of being locked away and closed in?
I don't know. But I do believe that all truly important works of art reflect and explain our world, our view of it.

What do you think about the quality of works by women writers in Latin America today?
I believe that many of them are extremely important for a special reason. You know, chamber music is less spectacular than a symphony, but it serves a function. That comparison applies to a feminine "chamber literature" that is absolutely extraordinary; it is fine, delicate, and with a visionary capacity that has achieved excellence in Latin America. The commercial writers interest me less than do those with exceptional sensitivity. One could easily name twenty women in Latin America of the Katherine Mansfield variety, truly splendid authors.

Why have we not heard about them then?
Have you ever heard of Latin American "machismo"? This is not a continent of men, but of "machos" who have eternally relegated woman to a secondary role, and when she has been able to take the reins up, she, too, has become a "macha," in a dominant role because of her wealth or her intelligence or commercial skill. But there are other women writers who do not enjoy those advantages and are considered subordinate and scorned even by male writers. Their work never appears in anthologies or in literary histories. It is as if they didn't exist. Look at Angel, whom I believe to be one of the critics who knows most about Latin American literature; he doesn't take the women into account. It's as if they didn't exist.

What's the solution then?
If two or three books of good, serious criticism by women were to appear; but the critical approach must be of the same quality as the literature itself. I don't believe there's been a woman writer like Rulfo or Cortázar or Guimaraes Rosa.

Not even Clarice Lispector?
Perhaps, Clarice. No, not even Clarice has written a novel like *Cien años de soledad* (*One Hundred Years of Solitude*).

But few male authors have written works to equal those by authors you've just mentioned.

Now that the "boom" frenzy has died down, I believe it is time to reflect more seriously on Latin American literature in order to discover its many faces.

Does the situation of the female author in Spanish America differ from that of the male author? Does she have the same opportunities to publish her work and circulate it in her own country? Abroad? In translations? The same opportunities to win national or international literary prizes?

She may have the same opportunities to publish her work as the male author but doesn't have the same opportunities for writing it. In her own country she can publish without great difficulty. Only a small group of writers are published abroad, in that group women rarely appear. The same holds true for translations. Women win national prizes when they're over seventy years old. She doesn't win international prizes unless she's a trite poet like Gabriela Mistral.

Are there certain taboo themes for women writers that would be accepted more easily by society if the author were a man?

I don't believe so. Women and men can work nowadays on any subject. Possibly the women writers don't go as far as the men in some instances, for example, in descriptions of the sexual act, because it doesn't interest them and they need not show any "machista" lack of inhibition.

In your fiction, do you consciously or subconsciously broach themes that specifically pertain to the Spanish American woman? Are you concerned with woman's socioeconomic role in Spanish America?

I broach them consciously. I don't know how to write except from my female perspective, with reference to all the themes that have concerned my generation and my children's generation.

138

Recently, have you been able to earn a living exclusively by writing fiction?

I would have died of hunger. I earn my living as an art critic and university professor. I've earned little with my fiction, but at least I have the satisfaction of never having paid for an edition nor of having solicited one. In all cases, the publishers have proposed publication to me.

What are you writing now? Does it sustain your interests expressed in earlier works? Are there new experiments, directions?

I'm finishing "La estación" (The Season), another brief novel about people who live in exile. Little by little the idea of a trilogy has matured: *Conversación al sur,* "La estación," and "Veinte años no es nada" (Twenty Years Is Nothing), a trilogy that, for now, would be entitled "La vida a cuestas" (Carrying Life Around). There is no other possible theme in my present writing than that of the life we began to carry around with us on our backs when it became impossible to return to our countries.

Presently, what kind of readings interest you most?

The foreign book that recently impressed me most is *Auto de fe* by Canetti. Of the Latin Americans, *La guerra del fin del mundo* (The War to End the World) by Mario Vargas Llosa, as well as other sagas, similarly apocalyptic in vision, like *El palacio de las blanquísimas mofetas* (The Palace of the Cadaverous Stench) by Reynaldo Arenas and *La vida entera* (Total Life) by Juan Carlos Martini. I, personally, have nothing in common with that world view because I'm a realist only tangentially, as is, for example, Jean Rhys; but it impresses me a good deal.

There are many Spanish American writers who do not live or have not lived at some time in their own countries but rather have written from abroad—for political, social, or personal reasons—in voluntary or involuntary exile: Cortázar, García Márquez, Vargas Llosa, Puig, Donoso. Does this situation apply to women writers from Spanish America? Do they feel the need or desire to distance themselves from their social context? Can they do so as easily as male authors?

The situation is the same. She finds it difficult to separate herself from her social context but that happens in the same way to a male writer. The problem of the diaspora and, at the center, the family's dispersion, destroys everyone equally. I believe no one *wants* to distance herself from her context, at least definitively. It happens as a fatality.

Since we met for the interview, have you written other books? Would you describe the importance you attach to your recently published fiction?

Homérica Latina is the most important book I've written. It is a desperate and poetic global attempt to relate, like a chronicle, man's terrible relationships with power. Few have seen it as such, but they will in time. Books are always discovered. *Conversación al sur* was my first successful book, which, taking into account my endorsement of Rilke's statement that "success is the sum of errors," doesn't make me lose my mind. Nevertheless, I believe its success is also due to the enormous task of organizing it into a symmetrical composition, conceived almost like a musical score, an atrocious theme expressed through the lives of two women. I didn't want to describe *a situation,* the death and disappearance of people in the Southern Cone, because I feel this is impossible; the situation will always surpass the dramatic level sought by the writer. This happened, for example, with the violence in Colombia. What I wanted was to explain how a particular situation damages and transforms one's life. I also wanted to show that women are the real heroines of this drama, though they didn't seem so at all. I believe I succeeded. The book is now appearing in Swedish and Norwegian translations, and this moves me because if you achieve something it is logical to want to share it with the greatest number of people.

Luisa Valenzuela

Argentina

But I am kaleidoscopic: my brilliant mutations fascinate me.

Clarice Lispector

Luisa Valenzuela. (Photo Sara Facio–Alicia D'Amico.)

Born in Buenos Aires, 1938. Mother, writer. Father, doctor. Raised in Belgrano. Taught by German governess and English tutor. Attended Belgrano Girls School, 1945. Attended an English high school. Began writing for the magazine *Quince Abriles*, 1953. Completed preparatory school education at National Preparatory School Vicente López, 1955. Began publishing in Buenos Aires magazines: *Atlántida, El Hogar, Esto Es;* worked with Jorge Luis Borges in the National Library; wrote for Belgrano Radio; worked as tour guide, 1957. Published first short stories in magazine *Ficción,* Buenos Aires; wrote for literary supplement *La Nación;* married French merchant marine Theodore Marjak; resided in Normandy; daughter Anna-Lisa born, 1958. Resided in Paris; wrote first novel, *Hay que sonreir;* wrote for Argentinian newspapers like *El Mundo* and for French radio broadcasts to Latin America; established contact with literary groups *Tel Quel* and the "new novel" movement, 1959–61. Returned to Buenos Aires; joined staff of *La Nación* Sunday supplement, 1961. Lectured throughout Argentina and other Latin American countries; held series of talks on literature for National Radio and Municipal Radio, 1962–68. Became assistant editor with *La Nación;* traveled to Brazil, 1964. Received subsidy from National Arts Foundation to publish *Hay que sonreír;* divorced husband, 1965. Won National Film Institute award for script "Clara" based on novel *Hay que sonreír;* traveled to Europe under invitation of governments of Great Britain, France, Italy, and Spain, 1966. Traveled throughout Argentina and to Lima and the Amazon region as correspondent for *La Nación,* 1968. Received Fulbright Fellowship to participate in International Writers Program at University of Iowa, 1969–70. Traveled and lectured in Mexico, Guatemala, Panama, Colombia, 1970. Returned to Argentina and journalistic work; embarked on lecture tour of Venezuela and Colombia supported by National Arts Foundation to develop cultural exchange program, 1971. Toured and lectured in Chile, Peru, Colombia, and Mexico; received grant from National Arts Foundation to study North American literature in the United States; resided in New York City for four months, 1972. Resided in Mexico and Barcelona, Spain, 1972–74. Returned to Buenos Aires; joined staff of magazine *Crisis,* 1975. Lectured throughout Mexico; invited to participate in Frankfurt Book Fair, 1976. Wrote for *Gente* magazine and literary supplement of *La Opinión* and *La Nación,* 1977. Conducted writers workshop at Universidad del Sur, Argentina; traveled to Ottawa, Canada, to participate in Inter-American Conference on Women Writers; left Buenos Aires and settled in New York, 1978. Conducted creative writing workshop in Spanish at Columbia University; lectured at Northwestern University, University of Wisconsin, Holy Cross, Pan American Society of New England, 1979. Fellow of the Institute for the Humanities of New York University, 1981–82. Member of Freedom to Write Committee of P.E.N. American Center, 1982. Guggenheim fellow; taught Latin American literature in writing division of Columbia University, 1983.

Luisa Valenzuela's narrative is revolutionary in two contradictory acceptations of the word: it reflects a violent break with tradition, future orientation, and change; and it evokes a time, cyclical in nature, like a planet revolving on its axis, a time in which myths are revealed and repeated. Valenzuela praises change and even consecrates herself to opening a breach in the complacent customs of the Western world. In doing this, she continues a modern tradition, born in Europe with Romanticism and in Spanish America of the late nineteenth century with "modernismo": the tradition of revealing society's inadequacies by slapping the middle class in the face—*épater le bourgeois.*

Focusing on eroticism and death in her fiction, Valenzuela transgresses taboos in a challenge to the bulwarks of modern societies in Spanish America: "almighty reason," rampant materialism, stifling social mores, the "fanaticism" of religion and politics, the socioeconomic hierarchies. In the wake of the destruction and desacralization leveled by her critical pen, she erects a universe of constant transformations that forces the reader to shed his self-sufficiency and invites him to confront the precarious nature of life. This existential vision is fused with a surrealistic style that emphasizes physical desire, and is fanned by a playful yet searing humor and irony. Valenzuela's writing becomes a search for identity: at once a carnival of masks that parody life and society and a ritualistic dance of purification and sacrifice.

Her subversive censure of an oppressive society manifests itself in a vitally constructive prose of incessant renovation and re-creation in which she irreverently pokes fun at social institutions. Nothing is spared. She satirizes Gallup polls, the married couple, organized religion, sex (machismo and virginity, the mystical sect of "telecoitus," and instructions for playing the game "fornicopula"), and high and pop cultures (soap operas, doctoral degrees, and semiotics). "Everything livable can be laughable," she explains.[1] With an incisive irony her short stories and novels tackle the political realities of Spanish

America—terrorism, persecution, torture, disappearances, dictator-ships—and some of their underlying socioeconomic causes, such as hunger, repression, the lack of dignity, and misery. In *El gato eficaz* ("The Efficient Cat"), the protagonist assures us, with tongue in cheek, that "satanism is no longer in vogue. Now the fad is goodness, good people, healthy motives and love-thy-distant-neighbor. It's all right to sigh for those who are starving but that's no reason to let them poke around in our pots. It's good to remind them that rice is healthier with the hull on and to leave them just that, the hull."[2]

Death, a constant in Valenzuela's fiction, stalks the starving masses and persists in every sexual encounter. Valenzuela adheres to many of Georges Bataille's ideas which link orgasm and death to religious expe-rience, taboo and transgression, desire and terror, and pleasure and anguish.[3] Eroticism embodies the violence and violation of death, a temporary negation of individuality on the part of two mortals who aspire to a fleeting union with eternity, the "little death" of an orgasm that erases for a moment their isolated existences: "If love is a little like death (a little death)," says a voice in *Como en la guerra* ("He Who Searches"), "death is pure love, the great cosmic orgasm."[4]

Loss of self in the erotic encounter, in death, or in writing is for Valenzuela the pursuit of otherness which wrenches one free from a spurious "omniscience" to achieve a more truthful polysemic and poly-morphic reality. The discourse of her third novel, *Como en la guerra,* is reflected and refracted as if by a mirror into many voices, conscious and subconscious and intimate and collective, whose kaleidoscopic transmutations challenge rational explanation. Her writing constantly responds to a mutable universe and so necessarily subverts language to communicate the only valuable reality, a protean "becoming." Thus, the word is demythified, exposed for its pretense, inadequacy, and incomprehensions: "i want to olev lions i want to hold a scalpel to cut my tongue every day i want i want i want not to belong to anything b cause belonging erases all possibilities for revolution t h atis the olny drue quality in man."[5]

Valenzuela's prose emphasizes free alterations in symbols, char-acters, structures, and style. Characters undergo corporal transforma-tions or encompass transsexuality, and her language is riddled with puns and word games. The eighteen chapters of Valenzuela's second novel, *El gato eficaz,* form a concatenation of the humorous, violent, and eschatological adventures of the female protagonist, an accomplice of the cats-of-death. She searches for somatic and semantic bliss, an eroticism of body and language, which is a constantly fluctuating state and the only hope for survival and renewal:

> Everything that tries to hold us back and detains us for a while is fatuous. The inalterable is fatuous with pretensions of eternity and not I who am not me myself I am transforming into colors on my retina, I gasify my shapes and keep on calling myself I, me, mine, not because of some old routine but rather for lack of something better and in the hope of a new comrade like you who may discover the keys to this game, line up the pieces—the white dogs-lives, the black cats-of-death—and renew the cycle. Checkmate again, may he smite me from afar. Smite me, imiteme, imitateme: my only hope lies in a rebirth.[6]

Perhaps the title of Valenzuela's second collection of short stories, *Aquí pasan cosas raras* (*Strange Things Happen Here*), best describes her imaginative prose, populated as it is by a gallery of marginal characters—prostitutes, peeping Toms, homosexuals—in an atmosphere of gothic horror or of mythic dimensions. Like her contemporary Julio Cortázar, Valenzuela lashes out to topple moral taboos. The playful quality and surrealistic flair of her fiction, however, do not diminish its social impact. Winking a jaundiced eye at the reader and flashing a great Cheshire cat grin, Valenzuela achieves uncanny, effective combinations in her satires, such as the following erotic parody of capitalist exploitation:

> She, on the other hand, was green like a Lorca poem and combed the vines of her body coursing with sap. Sap with chlorophyl, photosynthesis, a vegetable world decomposing until it becomes oil. And since there is never a scarcity of vampires—I repeat—she, too, met hers in spite of her metamorphoses.
> He was a rich Texan with a mighty fine ten-gallon hat who planted his rig deep down and sucked up the heaviest oils instead of irrigating her. A drill, that Texan, a real craftsman of wells even inside her. That's how he managed to extract a high percentage of combustible gases, a little bit of solvent. He could wrench from her a love that also burns, lose himself in petroputrid caresses.[7]

Buenos Aires, Argentina   *18 July 1978*

Do you belong to a specific generation of writers in Argentina?

I think we are all part of a literary generation and affected by certain influences. But in my time, unfortunately, I don't believe that there is a well-defined literary group. I say unfortunately because I would like to have been part of a group of creative people.

Do you feel an affinity with other Argentinian writers?

We all feel very independent and distant from one another. I don't think we would be the writers we are today if Borges had not existed first and Cortázar later. They completely altered our view of literature.

When did you begin to write fiction?

I wrote one solitary poem when I was six, and then when I was seventeen years old I wrote a short story. I had decided it wasn't so difficult to write stories the way a certain fashionable author of that time did. So I gave my story to Juan Goyanarte, who ran the magazine *Ficción*, and he published it. He was impressed and wanted me to write a novel. The revised version of the story called "Ciudad ajena" [The Foreign City] is now part of the book *Los heréticos* [The Heretics].

Which literary works have influenced you most in your career as a writer?

I don't know if any writer can answer that question. Personally, I cannot. Influences are so sporadic and aleatory. Everything that surrounds us, that occurs—music, science—influences one's writing.

Do you feel that any particular event in your life has influenced your writing more than another?

Of course. One thing that moved me and definitively transformed my art was my stay in New York. That scared me a great deal. Suddenly

El gato eficaz was born; it's very different from my other fiction. All of a sudden I touched vibrating passions with my fingertips and discovered that hatred and love are tactile.

The structure of your first novel, Hay que sonreír (Clara), *contrasts markedly with your later novels, like* El gato eficaz.

I wrote the first one in France when I was twenty-one years old. Later I polished it up a bit. Then I began to realize that the anecdote was less important than a profound philosophy about the subject and the language used to express it. Perhaps what I had been reading influenced me; later, I took the leap with *El gato eficaz.* It was not just the New York experience that motivated it but also a period of extreme solitude. I was in Iowa as a Guggenheim fellow, and all at once, I found myself alone, lonely like a mushroom, abandoned. From that encounter with myself a heap of internal ghosts emerged.

But let's return for a moment to that first novel, Hay que sonreír. *Why did you choose the life of a prostitute as the subject?*

There are lots of reasons. I think that all women believe in the prostitute. After all, she's the woman who possesses all men. At that time I lived in Paris, and the prostitutes lived in the same building I did. To my way of thinking they were very brave women because they used to get into cars and go with the men to the Bois de Boulogne Park across the way. It was courageous to get into a car with any old guy just to earn a few meager francs; after all, anything could have happened. I sympathized with those women, and when I heard their footsteps, I used to open the door for them. Sometimes they were running from the police to seek refuge in the building. I never talked with them, but a sort of remote understanding existed between us.

There are several traits in your early short stories, Los heréticos, *that evolve in your later novels. For example, the search for the unknown or for roots in the past reappears in* Como en la guerra (He Who Searches), *and many of these quests result in death.*

I feel that we usually follow a certain guiding thread which leads us through life. We don't lose that thread but sometimes we lose sight of it. So there could be a relationship between all of my searches because ultimately they are not the pursuit of death but of knowledge. Perhaps in the stories of *Los heréticos* the intent differed from that of the novel *Como en la guerra*. In the latter, one no longer perceives the idea that all religions are heretical simply because they take symbols literally. In *Como en la guerra* symbols *are* taken literally.

Were all the stories in Los heréticos *written about the same time?*

No. That's one of the defects of the book; the stories vary and were written at very different moments of my life. They lack unity. The idea of heresy has always interested me, and I return to it involuntarily. Right now, I'm interested in myths, that is, how myths originate; and I sense that literature may be a form of anthropological exploration (something which never occurred to me in *Los heréticos*, even though the subconscious idea may have been there).

The voyage and quest are fundamental to discovering life's hidden truths in El gato eficaz *and in* Como en la guerra. *They seem to signify both the flight from and the search for impossible personal love—and by extension death—in a sociopolitical sense. Would you explain the link between the voyage/search and collective societal goals in these two novels?*

There are no individuals who develop outside of their own society; and society is composed of individuals. What seems to be a personal goal is really everyone's battle, a collective quest. The individual search in its egotism is so very human that everyone partakes of it. All personal searches respond to numerous exigencies that many share. So the author may ask himself, "Why am I writing such a personal, egotistical work?" In fact, literature is neither exclusively self-centered nor intimate, for we are answering and formulating new questions that are universal preoccupations.

When you speak of redeeming oneself, what do you mean?

I ask myself that. Redeem oneself from all that has accumulated *against* ourselves or humanity or life. All we do is erect barriers, so possibly we ought not ask for forgiveness for good or bad deeds but rather for those which isolate us from each other.

One of the fundamental elements of Como en la guerra *is the mythical, archetypical exploration of reality. At times one notes a burlesque treatment of structuralism in the semiotics professor who dedicates himself to psychoanalyzing the prostitute, quotes Lacan, and whose interests are so all-encompassing that his very name, AZ, takes in the whole alphabet. In spite of this parody of a popular modern literary movement in criticism and linguistics, you seem to adhere to theories expounded by Lacan and Levi-Strauss, for example. Did you intend such a parody? What are your ideas about structuralism and Lacan's semiotics?*

I read Lacan before I began to write *Como en la guerra*. I spent a sleepless night reading Lacan. It was a great discovery for me. At the same time I joke about my great fascinations. Nothing is serious. I applied what I understood then about Lacan even though later I was to learn much more. That small bite of the Lacan "apple" opened many roads for me. What Lacan and the structuralists say about the subconscious and language, the signifier and signified, seems extraordinary to me. My literary research is based very much on the possibility of multiple significations for a signifier. It is an exploration of the word, the kind of prostituted word we use daily.

Is there no parody then?

Yes, there is a parody of Lacan who speaks in the first person plural form "we." He writes that way; it's a kind of infinite fatuity.

Pseudoscientific?

Yes, but suddenly he pulls your leg. And so do I. I'm not the keeper of truth nor do I pretend to be. That's why I foster ambiguity in my prose. The word is mine and possibly belongs to others, but not to everyone. So I invite you to read into that word whatever you will. Besides, a word has many connotations. Grab a dictionary; sometimes those meanings even contradict each other. I begin a sentence with a word meaning one thing, then all at once, in the middle of the sentence, the word begins to signify something else.

The passion and eroticism in your early stories like "Los heréticos," "La profesora" (The Professor), and "Una familia para Clotilde" (A Family for Clotilde) are also fundamental to your later works. Is there an evolution of these constants?

I believe that eroticism is very closely linked to language, to words laden with our own erotic desires. In the short stories, eroticism is seen from without as sin (that was my fault). Later on, eroticism is viewed more as communication with the divine. It is assumed and accepted by the author. There is an identification with eroticism. In the later works, *El gato eficaz* and *Como en la guerra,* there is no ethical judgment of eroticism.

In your fiction it appears that love is a synonym for intercourse, for death, sacrifice, and extermination, not only in El gato eficaz *but also in* Como en la guerra. *Would you clarify the source of this eroticism?*

I don't know whether or not I can explain that because it is complex. Love is a little death; they call an orgasm a "little death."

And why can't it be a "little bit of life"?

Because there is a contact with pain there, very close to desperation, a need to disintegrate into the other. It is also a vital experience; our way of denying death. Our Western and Judeo-Christian curse is the belief that death is horrible. I don't believe in the integration of souls but rather in the complete dispersion of the self. That is the most important thing one can do. For what reason would we preserve ourselves all tied up with strings? We have a dish in Argentina called *matambre.* It's beef rolled up and tied so the stuffing cannot ooze out. I run across people every day who remind me of *matambre,* all trussed up with strings. We're not *matambre;* we expand, transform, change.

There seems to be a sense of revenge between people in sexual relations, a sort of animal urgency—in the wolf-man, for example. Eroticism encompasses the transgression of taboos; there are peeping Toms, masturbators, lesbians, masochists, playful games, and symbolic sacrifices.

I don't know about the word revenge. Evidently these things happen at a very profound level where one is neither man nor woman. I was going to refer to the female reaction to male aggression. But I don't think that is even certain. Frankly, I don't know.

I'd like to know more about El gato eficaz. *Its genesis.*

El gato eficaz was a miracle. I was in Iowa as a fellow in the writer's program. In that place full of neurotic authors, I was very lonely. We writers are all neurotic and as individuals we can put up with ourselves; but in a group, it is much worse. We were under terrible stress, yet we were supposed to be creative. Months went by and no one was able to produce a sentence. And there we were, hysterical, playing pinball until about two in the afternoon. We had turned our daily schedules upside down. It was glorious; for example, it was snowing and frightfully cold, so we played "tropics" with the heat blasting as we danced to tropical music. At the same time we switched our routine so that we woke up at two in the afternoon and went to bed at five in the morning. In the midst of all that, at eleven one morning (daybreak for us), I awakened with an idea and a terrible need to write. I said to myself, "No, it can't be. I'll keep sleeping, this is ridiculous." But it persisted until finally that positive impulse won out (usually the negative one wins, the one that doesn't want me to write). So half asleep, I grabbed a notebook and began to write, and as I was writing, I thought, "How strange. This is weird and very interesting." But when one transcribes a dream, I thought, it always seems fascinating until later when you awaken and read it. Then it is a disaster, and you throw it in the trash. But I finished it thinking all along, "How can these ideas be occurring to me?" And sure enough, at two in the afternoon I woke up to discover that what I had written was very odd and interesting, the first three pages of *El gato eficaz*. I figured it was a short story; I read it to my friends who listened enthusiastically. And so the book poured forth like a waterfall, and I allowed it to flow without censoring that awesome relationship between love and death. I had not yet read Bataille. Later on I discovered how profound the material really was.

You wrote it all at once then?

I set it down everywhere. In the elevators of the building where we lived and in hamburger joints.

Did you revise it very much?

A little bit. You see, I have a theory that my subconscious functions very well so the work was already completed. There was some cacophony that needed to be changed. I felt that a certain rhythm had to be maintained and respected.

Is El gato eficaz *a novel?*

I consider it to be a novel because everything is a novel.

Everything?

Everything that has a certain form. I believe the word novel now includes many forms, its sense is broader nowadays.

But El gato eficaz *has a very fragmented structure. Why?*

We are fragmented; nothing is univocal; there is no unity. God is unity; we are pieces.

Most of the novel is narrated in the first person voice of the protagonist, but every once in a while an omniscient voice, apart from the action, provides a commentary. Why this perspective from beyond?

Every now and then I feel somewhat vain narrating in the first person, saying "*I* think this is *the* truth." The truth is neither here nor there, it is here *and* there. Possibly that perspective of a narrator behind another narrator is my way of setting things straight, but above all, of putting things in their place which is no place at all. Nothing is certain, nothing is a lie; everything is and is not, is outside and inside, and is positive and negative. Possibly it's a search for that "other truth."

The language in El gato eficaz *is filled with run-on words, partial words, neologisms,* lunfardo *slang. To what can we attribute your play-fulness with language?*

That was an approach to language which was more successful in *Como en la guerra.* It is a certain irreverent stand before language. Words are not so rigid; we have rendered them inflexible and emptied them of internal connotations. Words express much more than we want to say. So, in *El gato eficaz,* there is a sort of respectful disrespect, a need for words to belie their meanings but without allowing complete freedom. Neologisms don't interest me to the extent that simple words do.

As far as Como en la guerra *and* El gato eficaz *are concerned, what is your opinion of experimentalism in contemporary prose?*

Nothing should be forced; experimentation must respond to an intimate need. Then, of course, it is no longer experimental for it is simply another search.

Then it is a personal search in the realm of language, as well?

All novels, especially modern ones, question language in order to divest it of its crutches, to rejuvenate it, to make it more flexible, return to it an original vitality. Language communicates the writer's feelings and the reader's. Since I want each reader to undertake his own reading, I infuse language with a good dose of ambiguity.

What of the other games in El gato eficaz: *the inclusion of newspaper clippings, poems, outlines. To what extent are you pulling the reader's leg with the use of "pseudo" forms: pseudoscientific, pseudovirgin, pseudo-organized?*

Any jargon is a source of great entertainment. Pulling the reader's leg implies pulling my own; a true sense of humor begins at home with the author who can laugh at herself.

There are many parodies in El gato eficaz. *Is a criticism of society implied?*

Yes. It is the only way we are permitted to criticize any number of taboos.

You have written several political short stories. Can you explain to us the importance of politics and the often parodic treatment of it in your work?

With *Como en la guerra* we were seeing a very politicized period in Argentina; the novel captured that intensity. I think there is a message in that novel, and that's one of its defects. You see, we Argentinians feel ourselves to be Europeans, not very Latin American. But we *are* Latin American and we don't want to hear that.

In El gato eficaz, *it seems that all vital phenomena which are supposedly contrary to death—the-white-dogs-of-life, the spring, plants—still succumb to destruction like the cats-of-death themselves. The only difference seems to lie in the cyclical nature of life and death where the seasons or plants are concerned. In connection with such resurrections, you refer to "the splendorous fertility after the cataclysm, the primordial power of ashes."*

Of course, in *El gato eficaz* death is vital. That is, accepting death is fatal; the idea of eternity is a kind of constant death.

So then, life and death are similar, if not synonymous.

Very similar. It all came about in a strange way. We were discussing the fear of flying, and I boasted that I was not at all afraid of death,

154

that death was of no interest to me. And suddenly this terrible cascade poured forth from me, *El gato eficaz*. Evidently death is the human topic par excellence. But it is the theme of life. Without life there is no death; without death there is no life. By denying death we automatically deny life.

Would you discuss the omnipresent transformations in El gato eficaz?

Metamorphosis is a constant, and it is one of the things in life that disturbs me most. I try to instill constant change in those men who approach me. But people fear change. I, too, am afraid of it but cannot avoid it; I know it must be. Nothing is as it seems, everything is that and something more. So, onward, take heart. That's what Cortázar used to call walking along the edge of an abyss. If we are to walk, let's walk on the edge of a precipice knowing that something else lies beyond. Living is dying a little (so the song goes), but being conscious of death is existing intensely. Forgetting about death is like being a fruit compote in a refrigerator, in suspension, between parentheses.

Living intensely always implies change?

Yes. If we can, to the extent that we can, metamorphosis should persist; but almost always our changes are meager in comparison to our wishes. But it's worth a try.

In El gato eficaz *music—especially that of the flute, jazz, and song— bring about metamorphosis and erotic episodes.*

Yes, you see I once went to the village in New York where Herbie Mann was playing jazz flute. And in the middle of a number, all of a sudden I found myself standing on a chair howling with the black musicians who were going crazy. It was an electrifying experience, those notes that erupted from the vibraphone and the guitar. We all acted very strangely together. I believe that such a magical backdrop exists in literature, too. One reaches a state of the subconscious that Jung called collective. That flute moved me then. And many years later, a book appeared by a Bolivian named Taboada Terán, *Manchay Puytu, el amor que quiso ocultar Dios* [Manchay Puytu, the Love that God Tried to Hide]. It's the ancient Bolivian legend (which I never knew before) about a monk, a priest who was in love with an Indian woman and lived with her during the period of the Spanish conquest of

America. When the Indian woman died, the priest became desperate. He fashioned a flute from her tibia bone, and with the music it made, he resurrected her. That song is the Manchay Puytu; it has been prohibited in Bolivia for centuries. So you see how everything is linked together. A long time after I had written *El gato eficaz*, I read a book on Shamanism by Mircea Eliade about all kinds of magical rites among the Tibetans. And in *El gato eficaz*, such magical practices appear, too.

In El gato eficaz *there are amusing anecdotes, also, based on the exaggeration of the unusual. For example, the couple that must be separated in order to make love ends up founding the mystical sect of "telecoitus."*

I believe that a sense of humor is indispensable in literature, in life, in everything. Besides, there are small incidents that prompt the development of a theme.

In El gato eficaz, *alluding to the lame man, you say, "In pain and effort resides triumph." Do you feel one must suffer in order to attain certain ends?*

I don't know. I believe that one ought to take the right road, not always the easiest one. Facility impedes fidelity somehow.

Why is the tendency to corporal disintegration so great in that novel? Sometimes characters divest themselves of bodily parts or end up a bloody mass.

You know, I learned afterwards, while reading Jacques Lacan, about the ghost of the dismembered body. It seems that one of the forms of insanity involves the notion of imaginary anatomy that may be seen as whole, dismembered, or disintegrated. All those who reach beyond the threshold of reason view that imaginary anatomy as if it were foreign to their own bodies. Therefore, to a crazy person, the ghost of the dismembered body is one of the most important visions. I didn't know that when I wrote *El gato eficaz*.

So why did you write that way then?

My subconscious. Evidently we harbor this without realizing it. When I say crazy, I mean illuminated. I believe that religion is closely related to insanity; they are two faces of the same coin.

156

The mask and the disguise often play an important role in both El gato eficaz *and* Como en la guerra. *Would you comment on their significance in relation to transvestism, metamorphosis, and the revelation of death or clairvoyance?*

I cannot comment because I don't know. Whatever I know is in those texts, involuntarily. We wear a series of masks; we're never our deep, true, unique selves.

And transvestism?

Transsexuality as a theme fascinates me. I believe every human being is transsexual and the idea of a perfect, true sex is false. We all harbor both sexes; just as we have many masks, so we are both sexes only because there is no further choice.

What of the revelation of death or clairvoyance behind those masks or disguises?

Perhaps the only truth is death; it is the only moment of reintegration with the cosmos, of removing all masks. It lasts such a short time and afterwards becomes useless. That's its charm; it is a gratuitous act.

But at the end of Como en la guerra, *at least, the protagonist doesn't die.*

Well, not everyone has to perish.

Como en la guerra *and* El gato eficaz *could be considered surrealistic novels. In them, you esteem chance, exploration, dreams, nighttime, desire, imagination, exceptions to the rules, and that which is illogical, playful, and unusual. Surrealist symbols such as water and masks abound; there are constant metamorphoses; there is the Gothic horror of vampires, the attraction to murderers and the erotic, and woman as the key to the absolute. Some digressions from the surrealist novel can be seen in their fragmented points of view and their political messages.*

The surrealist movement really opened doors, whereas other interesting literary movements have closed doors, like the "new novel" in France. I don't believe in profoundly surrealistic, automatic writing. I believe in structuring prose. That's why Lacan is important to me, for he structures the subconscious. My "other," as Lacan would say, my subconscious, is infinitely more intelligent than I; and I believe that the human race is more intelligent than its individuals. We are social and political animals. And we are surrounded by a dogmatism (which I greatly fear) permitted by politics and religion. People who profess to dogmatic "truths" terrify me. We are innately political; we need to fight for a cause, an ideal, a hope.

Does the guerrilla theater in Como en la guerra *have anything to do with the Escambray group in Cuba?*
I don't know of that Cuban theater. No. It deals with some Argentinians who were putting on productions in the mines and with some Mexican friends whose puppet shows toured small villages exploring the local problems by narrating them in marionette theater. That way the villagers saw themselves mirrored in the productions. So the guerrilla theater in *Como en la guerra* is a great mixture of many experiences and my aspiration to create a dialogue with the people, offering them a mirror, the possibility of seeing themselves reflected so they can deduce their own answers.

In your fictional theater, a kind of anthropophagy occurs.
No, it doesn't.

It is suggested, though.
I believe that all love is anthropophagous.

What do you mean?
The problem is that love is anthropophagy.

Why?
There is a need to devour the other, to incorporate him into us. Anthropophagy is not only a form of cruelty but also a ritual form of making someone part of us by taking him into us bodily.

There seems to be an interesting balance between incorporating the other into us and giving of oneself to the other.
Yes. Good.

Because as you mentioned before, the "little death" is giving of oneself or losing isolation to gain continuity with the other for a moment.

But in our primitive villages, above all in the mountainous zones of Peru, the Inca empire regions of the high plateau, when a warrior or a great hunter died, they used to eat pieces of his flesh to recover his magical powers. They didn't kill him to eat him, but when he died, there was a need to physically incorporate his body into theirs in order to perpetuate his virtues. So that ritual anthropophagy conserves the greatness that the hunter represented.

I wonder if we could now turn to your opinion about the most important women authors today in Latin America?

I don't know if "important" is the right word to use because then I could mention the best known authors. But there are those that I esteem within a panorama of Latin America in general. For example, the Brazilian Nélida Piñón. She is a very serious writer who works with a profound literary knowledge. Albalucía Angel in Colombia is highly imaginative, very serious. Usually one believes that women write just to rid themselves of ghosts or other obsessions. But these are full-time authors.

Men also write to exorcise themselves. Why not women?

Because no great author writes just for that reason. Not women nor men. It would be too easy. No one rids himself of those ghosts anyway.

But there is an attempt, nevertheless.

All right. But gossip has it that women write a kind of diary to exorcise themselves, while men write as a kind of quest. It is not so. These women, and many others, write with a serious professionalism. The Colombian Albalucía Angel won a very important national prize (and justifiably so) and engaged in a fierce battle with her male compatriots. *Estaba la pájara pinta sentada en el verde limón* [The Speckled Bird Was Seated in the Green Lemon Tree] is an extraordinary novel. It has no sex. That is to say, it is an absolutely strong novel.

But, do novels have a sex?

Yes. Fortunately. Some are tremendously feminine and glorious.

I don't understand. What makes a novel feminine?

I think there is a feminine voice if a woman assumes her real voice, which can become very strong, very intense. For example, some of my mother's [Luisa Mercedes Levinson] novels are feminine. *La isla de los organilleros* (The Organ Grinders' Island) is written from a female perspective and yet has a certain force that many masculine novels would like to have. And there are many masculine novels that are not necessarily better than others because of that.

What characterizes a female novel and a male novel?

The subconscious has no sex, as we all know; it is transsexual. But, evidently all words cross through the barriers of our consciousness and are colored by it. There are men who have explored the feminine soul with a great deal of mastery but, in general, such an exploration into the profoundly aquatic and visceral world of women . . . well, I don't believe that a man could have written *El gato eficaz*. It is a view of eroticism from the female point of view. You know men can be tender, also, like women, but men don't allow themselves that trait. I feel sorry for men, at times, because they have to assume a role imposed on them since childhood: a strong man who ought not shed a tear, who should always perform sexually, and be the pillar of the family. Who'd want to do all that all the time? Why can't he be allowed to have weaknesses?

Such roles must be more rigid in Hispanic societies.

I think it's worse in the United States.

Why?

Because there it is a farce. The mask of machismo in Hispanic societies allows for certain weaknesses. But in your society, supposedly egalitarian, the North American business executive has to act like an executive who screws around. We at least have a definition for macho, but you don't, so it must be more difficult for men and for women. We, women, may undertake a complete rebellion but in your country there are many ways to rebel. It is more difficult because the means vary.

Are there certain characteristics, sensitivities, or themes which are more likely attributed to female fiction than to male?

More than themes, it is a question of sensitivities, or perhaps, the angle from which one approaches the same topic of interest to both sexes. I became conscious of this just a short while ago. I thought it was marvelous when they would tell me, "You write like a man." Now it's an insult. I realized that I didn't give a damn whether they said, "You write like a man" or "like a woman" or "like a tortoise." Besides, I believe that real strides will be made when we become more conscious of our true sexuality and write from the womb. I once had an argument with Salvador Elizondo during a radio broadcast in Mexico. While he was interviewing me, he asked, "Do you think there are female and male writers? I mean, feminine writers? Wait. Do you believe that women write in a feminine way and men in a virile manner?" So I answered him. "Look. Feminine and masculine, as you please. But they're not the same because if a man writes with his balls (scandalous on university radio in Mexico), then women have to write with their ovaries." He was taken aback but interested in the problem, and we did another show on another day. In the last analysis one must offer what one has to offer. We ought not pretend to have what we do not. We have internal reproductive sex organs. Why should we feign an alien form of sexuality, and why should we deny our own sexuality, which is just as strong or perhaps stronger than theirs?

But do you feel that physiological traits influence sociological phenomena?
Yes.

And sociological experience influences writing?
Yes. Absolutely. But I don't feel that we are inferior or less forceful or have fewer possibilities.

You believe, then, that there are some circumstances or situations with which women can deal and men cannot?
Yes. I believe that we are able to approach certain events that men cannot and vice versa.

Physiologically?
No. I'm referring to the exploration of language, of literature. The political power of a word, its ideological importance, is different for a man than for a woman. I feel that words possess power, they are charged with power which we have diluted and filed away so as to render words harmless. Society has done that. For example, the word "revolution" is used indiscriminately—a "revolution" of hairstyles. There are more subtle

examples which don't occur to me right now. One of the few duties of a writer is the restoration of the true meaning of words and the search for that which lies behind the myth: the transgression of the myth, its origin. It could be that a man's approach to these problems is not the same as a woman's. Perhaps the truth (I don't know if that's a good word), that is to say, the encounter with a certain form of reality, would be a combination of a man's and a woman's view. Not one or the other but the convergence of the two to render a truth.

Do you have any favorites among the women writers of Latin America?
Those I've already mentioned, and the Costa Rican Carmen Naranjo and the Venezuelan Antonieta Madrid.

And male writers?
One writer opened my eyes, and I continue to esteem him as a novelist: Samuel Beckett. Some of Cortázar's works. Arguedas interests me a lot right now.

Why?
I imagine because of his search into indigenous myths. Taboada Terán, also, the Bolivian. *Yo el supremo* [I Reign Supreme] by Roa Bastos, the Paraguayan, is an extraordinary novel; and the most important novel of these times is *Terra nostra* [*Terra nostra*] by Fuentes. It seemed to me a cosmogony, a marvelous, subtle, intelligent cosmovision, a game with time, space, and doubles. There is a sense of humor; it is well-written; the characters ring true. You piece together your own novel as you read along, discovering this very strange and complex plot like a puzzle. For me it is the most important novel of the seventies.

What do you think of the "boom" in Latin American literature?
There are marvelous books and very interesting writers who, all of a sudden, made people take note of literature as they never have before. But it was an exaggerated phenomenon.

What are you working on now?
A new novel. I just finished a book of short stories, and I also write for newspapers to stay in touch with life. So the saying goes. But I think that's just another pretense.

Does the situation of the female author in Spanish America differ from that of the male author? Does she have the same opportunities to publish her work and circulate it in her own country? Abroad? In translations? The same opportunities to win national or international literary prizes?

We artists, in general, tend to believe ourselves to be a special race, but this is only one more aspect of our illusions. For that very reason, a woman writer's situation is different from a man's, since it is a matter of one more reflexion of woman's place with respect to man. And I don't want to begin with complaints, that are not always so, about problems concerning publishing or being translated. No. I prefer to circumscribe my comments to a simple fact, which Tillie Olsen points out so well: a woman, who manages a house and raises children, lacks the free time so necessary for writing. And, above all, she lacks a wife to support her in everything and, if necessary, to act as her secretary. I believe that those are the basic problems, besides an undeniable lack of recognition on the part of the publishing house machinery in Hispanic America that separates us most from the Nobel Prize.

Are there certain taboo themes for women writers that would be accepted more easily by society if the author were a man?

What society accepts or rejects ought not concern the female writer. What cannot be said even by her because it remains censured in her dark subconscious—that is serious. They are the only truths worth being written. But women, who until recently were prohibited the use of so-called dirty language or harsh expressions, undoubtedly find it more difficult than men to transgress such barriers.

In your fiction, do you consciously or subconsciously broach themes that specifically pertain to the Spanish American woman? Are you concerned with woman's socioeconomic role in Spanish America?

This first answer to this question would be a flat "no." But since there is always a double game of mirrors, I think that unconsciously, it would be "yes." Undoubtedly, the problems of the Hispanic American woman worry me—not always the problems, many times I am amazed at her enormous fortitude—as do those of others in our countries who have no voice, even though they are so rich in perceptions.

Recently, have you been able to earn a living exclusively by writing fiction?

Let's say yes, but in the least creative aspects of literary tasks. I teach literature; I've been an author-in-residence at important institutions; I'm invited to conferences and write essays. There are very few people in this world who succeed in earning a good living by writing fiction exclusively. Of course, all the other benefits derive unquestionably from the fact that I write fiction, a crazy adventure that's fortunately very respected in this country where I've chosen to live. If I hadn't published books, I'd never be a university professor; I don't even have an Argentinian degree.

What are you writing now? Does it sustain your interests expressed in earlier works? Are there new experiments, directions?

I just finished a book of, let's say novellas. It's difficult to catalogue them, because in this case, though there is a close relationship between the four texts, the form varies and one cannot say if they are really short stories or novels. The title is *Cambio de armas* [Change of the Guard], and the theme is the ineffable, all that is not and cannot be said between a man and a woman. I've also written a small collection of poems that would be a new direction for me if it weren't that I consider them prose in truncated lines, as they say, the inverse of poems in prose. The real experiment will be, or perhaps is already, a work I'm planning on masks in which the fiction will be intimately linked to the essay, to the chronicle, or to mere information.

Presently, what kind of readings interest you most?

Scientific ones, as always.

There are many Spanish American writers who do not live or have not lived at some time in their own countries but rather have written from abroad—for political, social, or personal reasons—in voluntary or involuntary exile: Cortázar, García Márquez, Vargas Llosa, Puig, Donoso. Does this situation apply to women writers from Spanish America? Do they feel the need or desire to distance themselves from their social context? Can they do so as easily as male authors?

Woman is the mountain who must go to Muhammed. Therefore, no matter how much she may want or need to emigrate, even in questions of life or death, many times she cannot do so. She cannot leave her children behind, or she must follow her husband, or some other reason that society has invented for anchoring the reproductive uterus. Woman ought to be passive. Right? Of course. Luckily, the list of writers who are away from their respective countries is long and productive: Sara Gallardo, Cristina Perri Rossi, Albalucía Angel, Alicia Dujovne Ortiz, Helena Araújo, me. But this is also known as the diaspora. It would be interesting to be able to meet more often, not only every two or three years during the famous Congress of Inter-American Women Writers. Or, at least, have a publication that would put us in contact with one another.

Since we met for the interview, have you written other books? Would you describe the importance you attach to your recently published fiction?

Libro que no muerde [A Book That Doesn't Bite] is really a small anthology of short stories, some from 1966, others from 1976, and some new brief, almost philosophical reflections. As for "La hermana estrella o el señor de Tucuru" (or whatever this novel will ultimately be called), which Gregory Rabassa is now translating, I believe it to be my most ambitious work. They say that after the age of forty, a novelist truly matures. Well, here's the result. I think I've said some important things, but since I said them ironically, completely clothed in black humor, I don't know whether everyone will perceive them. For me, an Argentinian, it was the only way I could touch on a theme which would be too painful otherwise.

NOTES

Preface

1. Enrique Anderson Imbert and Eugenio Florit, *Literatura Hispanoamericana: Antología e introducción histórica*, 2 vols. (New York, 1960); Carlos Fuentes, *La nueva novela hispanoamericana* (Mexico, 1969); Julio Ortega, *La contemplación y la fiesta* (Lima, 1968); Emir Rodríguez Monegal, *Narradores de esta América*, vol. 1 (Montevideo, 1969), vol. 2 (Buenos Aires, 1974); Juan Loveluck, *Novelistas hispanoamericanos de hoy* (Madrid, 1976); Luis Harss and Barbara Dohmann, *Into the Mainstream: Conversations with Latin-American Writers* (New York, 1967); Rita Guibert, *Seven Voices* (New York, 1973).

2. María Luisa Bombal, *The Shrouded Woman*, anon. trans. (New York, 1948) and *The House of Mist*, anon. trans. (New York, 1946); Teresa de la Parra, *Mama Blanca's Souvenirs*, trans. Harriet de Onís (Washington, D.C., 1950).

3. Somers, "Madness" in *The Eye of the Heart: Short Stories from Latin America*, ed. Barbara Howes (Indianapolis and New York, 1973), pp. 300–302; Gambaro, "The Camp" in *Voices of Change in the Spanish American Theater*, ed. and trans. William I. Oliver (Austin and London, 1971), pp. 47–103; Lispector, *The Apple in the Dark*, trans. Gregory Rabassa (New York, 1967); and *Family Ties*, trans. Giovanni Pontiero (Austin, 1972); and Valenzuela, *Clara*, trans. Hortense Carpentier and J. Jorge Castelo (New York, 1976).

4. Jones, *Spanish American Literature in Translation*, 2 vols. (New York, 1963); Fremantle, *Latin American Literature Today* (New York, 1977); Monegal, *The Borzoi Anthology of Latin American Literature*, 2 vols. (New York, 1977); and Donoso and Henkin in the 1968–69 issue of *Tri-Quarterly*, which was later published as *The Tri-Quarterly Anthology of Contemporary Latin American Literature* (New York, 1969).

5. For example, the dissertations of Diane Solomon Birkemoe, "Contemporary Women Novelists of Argentina (1945–1967)," University of Illinois, 1968, and Martha Oehmke Loustaunau, "Mexico's Contemporary Women Novelists," University of New Mexico, 1973; Pescatello, *Female and Male in Latin America: Essays* (Pittsburgh, 1973).

6. These interviews resulted in my book *Cortázar por Cortázar* (Veracruz, 1978; 2nd. ed., 1981).

7. Wieser, ed., *Open to the Sun* (Van Nuys, Calif., 1979); Valenzuela, *Strange Things Happen Here,* trans. Helen Lane (New York, 1979); Meyer and Olmos, eds., *Contemporary Women Authors of Latin America,* 2 vols. (Brooklyn, 1983). Scattered selections include Julieta Campos, "Story of a Shipwreck," *Center for Inter-American Relations Review* 76, no. 18 (Fall 1976): 66–68; Nélida Piñón, "Bird of Paradise," *Review* 76, no. 19 (Winter 1976): 75–78; Clarice Lispector, "Sofia's Disasters," *Review* 24 (1979): 27–33; and Lygia Fagundes Telles, "New Fiction," *Review* 30 (September/December 1981): 65–70; Valenzuela, "The First Feline Vision," trans. from the novel *El gato eficaz* by Evelyn Picon Garfield, *Antaeus,* no. 48 (Winter 1983): 75–78; and Valenzuela, "The Best Shod" and "A Story about Greenery," *Ms* 7, no. 12 (June 1979): 60–61.

8. Resnick and de Courtivron, eds., *Women Writers in Translation* (New York, 1981); Knaster, *Women in Spanish America* (Boston, 1977).

9. *Latin American Women: Historical Perspectives* (Westport, Conn., 1978).

10. Edward B. Fiske, "Scholars Face a Challenge by Feminists," *New York Times,* 23 November 1981, p. 12.

11. Harold C. Schonberg, "Hispanic Impact on the Arts: Mysticism to Machismo," *New York Times,* 13 December 1981: 1, 32.

12. Boyd G. Carter, *Las revistas literarias de Hispanoamérica* (Mexico, 1959), p. 167.

Introduction

1. Matei Calinescu, *Faces of Modernity* (Bloomington, Ind., 1977), p. 10. For a theoretical discussion of the Age of Modernity as it applies specifically to Latin America see Evelyn Picon Garfield and Ivan A. Schulman, *"Las entrañas del vacío": Ensayos sobre la modernidad hispanoamericana* (Mexico City, 1984).

2. Willis Knapp Jones (*Spanish American Literature in Translation* [New York, 1963], p. 208) quotes a famous one:

> Stupid men, quick to condemn
> Women wrongly for their flaws,
> Never seeing you're the cause
> Of all that you blame in them!

3. Translated by Yvonne Guillon Barret in an unpublished manuscript.

4. "Our America" in *The America of José Martí,* trans. Juan de Onís (New York, 1953), p. 146.

5. Daniel Bell, *The Cultural Contradictions of Capitalism* (New York, 1976), p. 13.

6. Irving A. Leonard, *Baroque Times in Old Mexico* (Ann Arbor, Mich., 1959), pp. 225–26.

7. For further discussion of this subject see Ivan A. Schulman, "Introduction to the English Edition: In Pursuit of a Literature" in *Latin America in Its Literature* (New York and London, 1980), pp. 27–35.

8. *Los hijos del limo* (Barcelona, 1974), p. 60.

9. Ibid., p. 37.

10. A term used in the title of an article by Angel Rama, "Raros y malditos en la literatura uruguaya," *Marcha* (Montevideo) no. 1319 (September 1966): 31.

11. For a discussion of the "open work" see Umberto Eco, *Opera aperta* (Milan, 1962).

12. "Prólogo a *El poema del Niágara*" in José Martí, *Páginas Escogidas,* selection and prologue by Roberto Fernández Retamar, vol. 2 (Havana, Cuba, 1965), p. 169.

13. "Novela de la conciencia y conciencia de la novela," *Plural* (Mexico City) no. 35 (August 1974): 72.

14. Rama, "Raros y malditos," p. 31.

15. *Imaginación y violencia en América* (Santiago, Chile, 1970).

16. "The Passion According to G. H." in Emir Rodríguez Monegal, *The Borzoi Anthology of Latin American Literature* (New York, 1977), pp. 781–82.

17. Interview with E. P. Garfield, 1978.

Armonía Somers

1. Angel Rama, "La fascinación del horror," *Marcha* (Montevideo), no. 1188 (27 December 1963): 30.

2. Angel Rama, "Raros y malditos," *Marcha* (Montevideo), no. 1319 (1966): 30–31.

3. *De miedo en miedo*, p. 88.

4. All quotations, unless specified otherwise, are part of the interview the author held with Armonía Somers in Montevideo on 14 July 1978.

5. *De miedo en miedo*, p. 52.

6. Ibid., p. 61

7. *Todos los cuentos 1953–67*, vol. 2, pp. 93, 66.

8. Ibid., vol. 1, p. 89.

9. Ibid., p. 46.

10. Enrique Raab, "Amor y vida de mujer," *Confirmado* (Montevideo) 3, no. 123 (26 October 1967): 44.

11. *Todos los cuentos 1953–67*, vol. 2, p. 125.

12. Ibid., vol. 1, p. 55.

13. *De miedo en miedo*, p. 98.

14. *Todos los cuentos 1953–67*, vol. 1, p. 17.

15. Ibid., p. 85.

Griselda Gambaro

1. *Dios no nos quiere contentos*, p. 250.

2. *El campo*, pp. 28–29.

3. Ibid., p. 53.

4. Ibid., pp. 34–35.

5. *Dios no nos quiere contentos*, p. 104.

6. Ibid., pp. 126, 178, 85, 249.

7. Ibid., p. 63.

Julieta Campos

1. "La imagen en el espejo" in *La imagen en el espejo*, p. 73.

2. "¿Tiene sexo la escritura?" *Vuelta* (Mexico City) no. 21 (August, 1978): 45.

3. "Todas las voluntades caben," *Vuelta* (Mexico City) no. 22 (September, 1978): 51.

4. *Función de la novela*, p. 31.

5. "La novela de ausencia" in *La imagen en el espejo*, p. 41.

6. Campos in an interview with Josefina Millán, "La literatura: Esa memoria donde convergen todas las memorias," *Excelsior* (Mexico City) 2 February 1975, p. 6.

7. Julio Cortázar, *Hopscotch*, trans. Gregory Rabassa (New York, 1966), pp. 373–74.

8. Eco, *Opera aperta*.

9. "Todas las voluntades caben," p. 52.

10. Millán, "La literatura," p. 6.

11. *El miedo de perder a Eurídice*, p. 17.

12. "¿Tiene sexo la escritura?" p. 45.

Elvira Orphée

1. All quotations, unless otherwise indicated, are from the interview the author held with Orphée in Buenos Aires on 17 July 1978.

2. *La última conquista de el Angel*, p. 109.

3. "La calle Mate de Luna" (Mate Luna Street) in *Su demonio preferido* (Her Favorite Demon), p. 27.

4. Yukio Mishima, *The Decay of the Angel*, trans. Edward G. Seidensticker (New York, 1974), p. 14.

5. "Elvira Orphée: Escritura con complejos," *Usted*, no. 31 (23 May 1961): 21.

6. "Los demonios de lo cotidiano," *La Opinión Cultural*, (27 November 1977): 10–11.

7. *Aire tan dulce*, p. 260.

8. Jorge Luis Borges, *Otras inquisiciones* (Buenos Aires, 1960), p. 144.

Marta Traba

1. *Pasó así*, p. 127.

2. *Conversación al sur*, p. 167.

3. Ibid., p. 46.

4. Ibid., pp. 166–67.

5. Ibid., pp. 45–46.

6. Ibid., p. 87.

Luisa Valenzuela

1. *El gato eficaz*, p. 67.

2. Ibid., p. 11.

3. Georges Bataille, *Death and Sensuality: A Study of Eroticism and the Taboo* (New York, 1962), p. 39.

4. In *Strange Things Happen Here,* p. 196.

5. *El gato eficaz,* p. 107.

6. Ibid., p. 119.

7. Ibid., p. 110.

BIBLIOGRAPHIES

Armonía Somers

Fiction

"La mujer desnuda." *Clima* (Montevideo) no. 2, 1st ed., 1950; 2nd ed., 1951.

La mujer desnuda. Montevideo, 1967.

El derrumbamiento. Montevideo, 1953.

La calle del viento norte. Montevideo, 1963.

De miedo en miedo (Los manuscritos del río). Montevideo, 1965; two short stories of which appeared as "Madness" in *The Eye of the Heart: Short Stories from Latin America,* edited by Barbara Howes, pp. 300–302, Indianapolis and New York, 1973; and as "The Immigrant," translated by Anne Hohenstein in *Diana's Second Almanac,* pp. 4–35, Providence, R.I., 1980.

Todos los cuentos 1953–67. 2 vols. Montevideo, 1967.

Un retrato para Dickens. Montevideo, 1969.

Muerte por alacrán. Buenos Aires, 1978.

Tríptico Darwiniano. Montevideo, 1982.

Sólo los elefantes encuentran mandrágora. Buenos Aires. Forthcoming.

Short Works

Short stories and prefaces in *Enciclopedia Uruguaya,* no. 3, 1968, *Maldoror, El País, Caravelle* (France), and *La vida literaria* (Mexico City).

Postscript to *Diez relatos y un epílogo.* Montevideo, 1979, pp. 113–54.

173

Secondary Sources

Alvarez, José Carlos. "*De miedo en miedo:* Con Armonía Somers." *La Mañana* (Montevideo), 31 December 1965.

Araújo, Helena. "Escritura femenina: Sobre un cuento de Armonía Somers." *Cuéntame tu vida* (Cali, Colombia) no. 5, (1981): 19–24.

"Armonía Somers." *Cahiers du Monde Hispanique et Luso-Bresilien (Caravelle)* (Toulouse, France) no. 24 (1975).

"Armonía Somers: Los lobos esteparios." *Capítulo Oriental,* no. 33 (1968): 523.

"Armonía Somers: *Todos los cuentos 1953–1967.*" *Extra* (Montevideo), 4 July 1967.

Benedetti, Mario. Review of *El derrumbamiento. Número* (Montevideo) 5, no. 22 (January–March 1953): 102–3.

———. "*La calle del viento norte:* Cinco cuentos para que el hombre se acuerde de la muerte." *La Mañana,* no. 16325 (1964).

———. *Literatura uruguaya siglo XX.* 2nd ed., Montevideo, 1969.

Carbajal, Miguel. "Armonía Somers o el escándalo del talento." *El Debate,* Supplement B (Montevideo), 3 May 1970.

Cotelo, Rubén. *Narradores uruguayos.* Caracas, 1969, pp. 149–70.

Couste, Alberto. "Armonía Somers, Al este del paraíso." *Primera Plana* (Buenos Aires) no. 242 (1967): 52–53.

De Espada, Roberto. "La ferozmente amada orilla del mundo." *De Frente* (Montevideo), 31 March 1970.

———. "*Un retrato para Dickens* por Armonía Somers." *Ya* (Montevideo), 29 June 1970.

———. "Armonía Somers o el dolor de la literatura." *Maldoror* (Montevideo), 1st trimester (1972): 62–66.

"El autor frente a su público: Armonía Somers." *Tribuna Salteña* (Montevideo), 1969.

Figueira, Gastón. "Nuestra literatura femenina en el último cuarto de siglo." Supplement of *La Mañana,* no. 1327 (1961).

———. Review of *La calle del viento norte. Books Abroad* (Summer 1964): 295.

Fornaro, Milton. "Armonía Somers, una auténtica narradora." *El Día* (Montevideo), 17 June 1978.

García Rey, Juan Manuel. "Maldición y exorcismo, veintiuna preguntas a Armonía Somers." *Sintaxis* (Montevideo), April 1978.

Garfield, Evelyn Picon. "Yo soplo desde el páramo: La muerte en los cuentos de Armonía Somers." *Texto crítico* (Veracruz) no. 6 (January–April 1977): 113–25.

Gilio, María Ester. "A cada cual su ración de amor" (interview). *Marcha,* no. 1298 (1966).

———. "El Rosario de Eros." *El País* (Montevideo), 12 July 1966.

Glantz, Margo. "Djuna Barnes y Armonía Somers: ¿Tiene la escritura sexo?" *Sábado.* Supplement of *Uno más uno* (Mexico City), 6 July 1980.

Hohenstein, Anne. Ph.D. diss. in progress on A. Somers, Brown University.

"La narrativa femenina." *Capítulo Oriental,* no. 34 (1968): 540–41.

"La segunda vida de Oliverio Twist." *Periscopio* (Buenos Aires) no. 26 (17 March 1970): 45.

Merica, Ramón. "La armonía de todas las horas." *El País* (10 February 1968): 7–8.

Paganini, Alberto, Alejandro Patermain, and Gabriel Saad. *Cien autores del Uruguay,* no. 45. Argentina, 1969.

Penco, Wilfredo. "Armonía Somers, el mito y sus laberintos." *Noticias* (Montevideo) no. 82 (October 1979): 50–52.

Pérez Senac, J. Román. "*El derrumbamiento*, Armonía Somers." Supplement of *La Mañana*, 10 August 1953.

Raab, Enrique. "Amor y vida de mujer." *Confirmado* (Buenos Aires) no. 123 (1967): 44.

Rama, Angel. "Testimonio, confesión y enjuiciamiento de veinte años de historia y de nueva literatura uruguaya." *Marcha* (Montevideo), 1960.

———. "La insólita literatura de Somers: La fascinación del horror." *Marcha*, no. 1188 (1963): 30.

———. "Mujeres, dijo el penado alto." *Marcha*, no. 1290 (1966).

———. *Cien años de raros*. Montevideo, 1966, p. 11.

———. "Raros y malditos en la literatura uruguaya." *Marcha*, no. 1319 (1966): 30–31.

———. *La generación crítica 1939–1969*. Montevideo, 1972.

———. "La conciencia crítica." *Enciclopedia Uruguaya*, no. 56. Montevideo, 1969.

Rufinelli, Jorge. "Paraíso infernal, celeste infierno." *Marcha*, no. 1378 (10 November 1967).

———. "Historia de ángeles y demonios." *Marcha* (30 January 1970): 29.

Schell, Corina. "Armonía Somers en Punta del Este." *Punta del Este* (Montevideo) no. 4738 (24 January 1968): 1, 9.

"Testimonio: Una gran escritora uruguaya (A.S.) habla para *Rumbos*." *Rumbos* (Montevideo) 1, no. 1 (3 October 1969): 8–9.

"Un tránsito de muertes." *Extra* (3 September 1967).

Villafañe, Jorge E. "Armonía Somers, *La mujer desnuda*." *La Mañana*, (1952).

Visca, Arturo Sergio. *Antología del cuento uruguayo: los nuevos*. Montevideo, 1968.

———. "La obra narrativa de Armonía Somers." *El País* (30 September 1969).

———. "Un enigmático dibujo." *El País* (11 January 1970).

———. "El mundo narrativo de Armonía Somers." In *Nueva antología del cuento uruguayo*. Montevideo, 1976.

Vitale, Ida. "Una autora singular: Armonía Somers." *Epoca* (Montevideo) no. 541 (1963).

———. "Cinco preguntas semanales, contesta Armonía Somers." *Epoca* 1, no. 338 (23 May 1963).

Zum Felde, Alberto. *Indice crítico de la literatura hispanoamericana*. Vol. 2, *La narrativa*. Mexico City, 1959; 2nd ed., Madrid, 1964, p. 501.

Griselda Gambaro

Plays Published

El desatino. Buenos Aires, 1965.

Los siameses. Buenos Aires, 1967.

El campo. Buenos Aires, 1967 and 1981; appeared as "The Camp" in *Voices of Change in the Spanish American Theater*, edited and translated by William I. Oliver, pp. 47–103. Austin and London, 1971.

"La gracia." *El Urogallo*, no. 17 (1972).

"Sólo un aspecto." *La Palabra y el Hombre*, no. 8 (1973).

"Decir Sí." *Hispamérica*, no. 21 (1978); and *Antología Teatro Abierto*. Buenos Aires, 1981.

Teatro: Las paredes, El desatino, Los siameses. Barcelona, 1979.

Nueve dramaturgos hispanoamericanos (*Los siameses*). Ottawa, 1979.

"El despojamiento." *Tramoya*, nos. 21–22, (November–December 1981).

Plays Performed

"Matrimonio." Buenos Aires, 1965.

Las paredes. Buenos Aires, 1966.

El desatino. Buenos Aires, 1966.

Los siameses. Buenos Aires, 1967.

El campo. Buenos Aires, 1968.

"Nada que ver." Buenos Aires, 1972.

"Sólo un aspecto." Buenos Aires, 1974.

"El viaje." Buenos Aires, 1975.

"El nombre." Buenos Aires, 1976.

"Sucede lo que pasa." Buenos Aires, 1976.

"Decir Sí." Buenos Aires, 1981.

"La Malasangre." Buenos Aires, 1982.

Many of these plays have also been staged abroad, especially *The Camp*, in France, Italy, Germany, Poland, Mexico, Venezuela, Uruguay, and the United States.

Fiction

Madrigal en ciudad. Buenos Aires, 1963.

El desatino. Buenos Aires, 1965.

Una felicidad con menos pena. Buenos Aires, 1967.

Nada que ver con otra historia. Buenos Aires, 1972.

Ganarse la muerte. Buenos Aires, 1976; French trans., 1976.

La cola mágica (stories for children). Buenos Aires, 1976.

Dios no nos quiere contentos. Buenos Aires, 1979; French trans., 1983; Polish trans. forthcoming.

Nonfiction

Conversaciones con chicos. Buenos Aires, 1976.

"¿Es posible y deseable una dramaturgia específicamente femenina?" *Latin American Theatre Review* (Summer 1980): 17–22.

Short Works

Essays, short stories, and reviews in *Ficción, Análisis, Mantrana, Revista de la Universidad Nacional del Litoral, Clarín, Talía, El cronista, La Opinión, La Nación, Teatro Municipal, Vigencia,* and *Sipario* (Milan).

Secondary Sources

Arlt, Mirta. "Griselda Gambaro: La verdad tiene cara de absurdo." *Revista Lyra,* nos. 231–33 (December 1976).

Azcona Cranwell, Elizabeth. Review of *Una felicidad con menos pena. Sur,* no. 315 (November–December 1968): 92–94.

Boorman, Joan Rea. "Contemporary Latin American Women Dramatists." *Rice University Studies* 64, no. 1 (1978): 69–80.

Carballido, Emilio. "Griselda Gambaro o modos de hacernos pensar en la manzana." *Revista Iberoamericana*, no. 73 (October–December 1970): 629–34.

Cárrega, Hemilce. "*Una felicidad con menos pena.*" *La Prensa* (28 September 1968).

Cruz, Jorge. "La obsesión de la crueldad." *La Nación* 192 (September 1976).

Cypess, Sandra Messinger. "Physical Imagery in the Plays of Griselda Gambaro." *Modern Drama* 18, no. 4 (December 1975): 357–64.

———. "The Plays of Griselda Gambaro." In *Dramatists in Revolt: The New Latin American Theatre,* edited by George W. Woodyard and Leon F. Lyday, pp. 95–107. Austin, 1976.

De Moor, Magda Casteellvi. "El vanguardismo en el teatro hispánico de hoy: Fuentes, Gambaro y Ruibal." Ph.D. diss., University of Massachusetts, 1980.

Dujovne Ortiz, Alicia. "Así es, si os parece." *La Nación* (9 April 1972): 14–15.

Echagüe, Selva. "Griselda Gambaro: Escribir me justifica." *Clarín* (2 March 1972): 13.

Feiman Waldman, Gloria. "Three Female Playwrights Explore Contemporary Latin American Reality: Myrna Casas, Griselda Gambaro, Luisa Josefina Hernández." In *Latin American Women Writers: Yesterday and Today,* edited by Yvette Miller and Charles M. Tatum, pp. 75–84. Pittsburgh, 1977.

Flynn, Susan Kingston. "The Alienated Hero in Contemporary Spanish American Drama." Ph.D. diss., University of Illinois at Urbana-Champaign, 1977.

Ford, Aníbal. "La realidad histórica se diluye en la última obra de Griselda Gambaro." *La Opinión* (26 December 1972).

Foster, David William. "El lenguaje como vehículo espiritual en *Los siameses* de Griselda Gambaro." *Escritura* 4, no.8 (July–December 1979): 241–57.

———. "The Texture of Dramatic Action in the Plays of Griselda Gambaro." *Hispanic Journal* 1, no. 2 (1979): 57–66.

Foster, Virginia Ramos. "The Buenos Aires Theater, 1966–67." *Latin American Theater Review,* no. 1/2 (Spring 1968): 58.

———. "Mario Trejo and Griselda Gambaro: Two Voices of the Argentina Experimental Theater." *Books Abroad* 42, no. 4 (Autumn 1968): 534–35.

Garfield, Evelyn Picon. "Una dulce bondad que atempera las crueldades: *El campo* de Griselda Gambaro." *Latin American Theatre Review,* Supplement, no. 13/2 (Summer 1980): 95–102; augmented version in *Zona Franca* (Caracas) 3, no. 19 (July/August 1980): 28–36.

Holzapfel, Tamara. "Griselda Gambaro's Theatre of the Absurd." *Latin American Theatre Review* (Fall 1970): 5–12.

Karvelis, Ugné. "L'enfer de Cledy." *Littéraire Le Figaro* (14–15 December 1976).

Kiss, Marilyn Frances. "The Labyrinth of Cruelty: A Study of Selected Works of Griselda Gambaro." Ph.D. diss., Rutgers University, 1982.

Lima, Dora. "Una obra nacional en el Agón." *El mundo* (17 April 1966).

M. B. "El revés del absurdo." *Confirmado* (24 October 1968).

Moretta, Eugene L. "Spanish American Theatre of the 50's and 60's: Critical Perspectives on Role Playing." *Latin American Theatre Review* 13, no. 3 (1979): 5–30.

Muxó, David. "La violencia del doble: *Los siameses* de Griselda Gambaro." *Prismal/Cabral* 2 (1978 Spring): 24–33.

Podol, Peter L. "Reality Perception and Stage Setting in Griselda Gambaro's *Las paredes* and Antonio Buero Vallejo's *La fundación.*" *Modern Drama* 24, no. 1 (March 1981): 44–53.

Sáenz, Jorge Luis. "*El campo* de Griselda Gambaro." *Sur,* no. 315 (November–December 1968): 121–22.

Schóó, Ernesto. "Teatro, Griselda Gambaro: El creador, un hombre como todos." *Confirmado* (4 April 1972): 42–44.

Zalacaín, Daniel. "Marqués, Díaz, Gambaro: Temas y técnicas absurdistas en el teatro hispanoamericano." Ph.D. diss., University of North Carolina at Chapel Hill, 1976.

———. "El personaje 'fuera del juego' en el teatro de Griselda Gambaro." *Revista de Estudios Hispánicos* 14, no. 2 (1979): 59–71.

Julieta Campos

Fiction

Muerte por agua. Mexico, 1965; 3rd ed., 1978.

Celina o los gatos. Mexico, 1968.

Tiene los cabellos rojizos y se llama Sabina. Mexico, 1974; 2nd ed., 1978.

"Historia de un naufragio." Mexico, 1976; appeared as "Story of a Shipwreck," translated by Beth Miller in *Center for Inter-American Relations Review* 76, no. 18 (Fall 1976): 66–68.

El miedo de perder a Eurídice. Mexico, 1979.

Literary Theory and Criticism

La imagen en el espejo. Mexico, 1965.

Oficio de leer. Mexico, 1971.

Función de la novela. Mexico, 1973.

"¿Tiene sexo la escritura?" *Vuelta* 2, no. 21 (August 1978): 44–45.

La herencia obstinada. Mexico, 1982.

Secondary Sources

Batis, Humberto. "Los libros al día." *La Cultura en México* (9 February 1966): 16.

B. R. N. "Julieta Campos." *Siempre,* no. 214 (23 March 1973).

Francescato, Martha P. "Un desafío a la crítica literaria: *Tiene los cabellos rojizos y se llama Sabina* de Julieta Campos." *Revista de Crítica Literaria Americana* 7, no. 13, 1st semester (1981): 121–25.

Garfield, Evelyn Picon. Review of *Tiene los cabellos rojizos y se llama Sabina. Revista Iberoamericana,* nos. 112–13 (July–December 1980): 680–83.

———. "*Tiene los cabellos rojizos y se llama Sabina* de Julieta Campos: Una caída interminable en la inmovilidad." *Eco* (Bogotá), no. 248 (June 1982): 172–91.

Glantz, Margo. "Entre lutos y gatos: José Augustín y Julieta Campos." In *Repeticiones, Ensayos sobre literatura mexicana,* pp. 70–74. Xalapa, Mexico, 1979.

Millán, Josefina. "La literatura: Esa memoria donde convergen todas las memorias." *Excelsior* (2 February 1975): 6–7.

Miller, Beth. "Julieta Campos: La escritura es un modo de organizar la vida." *Los Universitarios* (1974): 6–8.

———. "Julieta Campos" and "Entrevista con Julieta Campos." In *Mujeres en la literatura,* pp. 118–27. Mexico, 1978.

Osorio, Lilia. "Julieta Campos, Mientras alguien voraz a mi me observa." *Siempre,* 1974.

Pacheco, José Emilio. "Novela de la conciencia y conciencia de la novela." *Plural,* no. 35 (August 1974): 72–73.

Rodríguez Nebot, Joaquín. "Una herencia y su historia" (Review of *La herencia obstinada*). *Revista de la Universidad de México* 38, no. 20 (December 1982).

Verani, Hugo J. "Julieta Campos y la novela del lenguaje." *Texto Crítico* 2, no. 4 (1976): 132–49.

Young, Rinda Rebeca Stowell. "Six Representative Women Novelists of Mexico, 1960–69." Ph.D. diss., University of Illinois at Urbana-Champaign, 1975.

Elvira Orphée

Fiction

Dos veranos. Buenos Aires, 1956.

Uno. Buenos Aires, 1961.

Aire tan dulce. Buenos Aires, 1966; 2nd ed., Caracas, 1977.

En el fondo. Buenos Aires, 1969.

Su demonio preferido. Buenos Aires, 1973.

La última conquista de el Angel. Caracas, 1977.

Las viejas fantasiosas. Buenos Aires, 1981.

Short Works

Short stories and articles published in *El Tiempo* (Bogotá), *Cuadernos* (Paris), *Asomante* (Puerto Rico), *Razón y Fabula* (Bogotá), *Revista de Occidente* (Madrid), *Zona Franca* (Caracas), *Imagen* (Caracas).

Secondary Sources

A. C. "*Uno,* novela de Elvira Orphée." *Ficción,* no. 32 (July–August 1961): 78.

Alonso, Rodolfo. Review of *Aire tan dulce. La Gaceta* (Tucumán) (16 July 1961).

———. "Polémica sobre *Uno:* Carta abierta a David Lagmanovich." *La Gaceta* (16 July 1961).

Alvarez Sosa, Arturo. "*Su demonio preferido.*" *La Gaceta* (8 July 1973): 2.

Baracchini, Diego. "El retrato inalcanzable de Elvira Orphée." *La Opinión* (15 January 1978): 21.

Bastos, María Luisa. Review of *Uno. Sur,* no. 272 (September–October 1961): 107–9.

———. "Una escritora argentina: Elvira Orphée." *Zona Franca* (Caracas) 3, no. 44 (April 1967): 24–26.

———. "Silencios comunicantes." *La Nación* (1967).

———. "Tortura y discurso autoritario: *La última conquista de el Angel* de Elvira Orphée." In *The Contemporary Latin American Short Story,* edited by Rose S. Minc. New York, 1979.

Chacel, Rosa. "Un libro ciertamente nuevo." *Sur,* no. 245 (March–April 1957): 111–17.

Chevigny, Bell. "Ambushing the Will to Ignorance: Elvira Orphée's *La última conquista de el Angel* and Marta Traba's *Conversación al sur.*" In *El cono sur: Dinámica y dimensiones de su literatura,* edited by Rose S. Minc. Upper Montclair, N.J., 1985, pp. 98–104.

"Conversación con Elvira Orphée." *Zona Franca* 3, no. 2 (July–August 1977): 24–28.

Correa, María Angélica. Review of *Uno. Señales,* no. 131 (July–August 1961): 29.

Crespo, Julio. "*Aire tan dulce.*" *Sur,* no. 307 (July–August 1967): 47–49.

Da Silva, Carmen. Review of *Uno. Entrega* (Buenos Aires) (1961).

De Olaso, Ezequiel. "*Uno.*" *La Nación* (4 July 1961).

Dujovne Ortiz, Alicia. "Una peligrosa intimidad." *Clarín* (1973).

———. "Los demonios de lo cotidiano." *La Opinión Cultural* 27 (November 1977): 10–11.

E. D. Review of *Dos veranos. Ficción,* no. 4 (November–December 1956): 192–94.

"El espantoso amor." *La Nación* (13 November 1977).

"Elvira Orphée: Escritora con complejos." *Usted,* no. 31 (May 1961): 21.

"Elvira Orphée." *La Nación* (April 1975).

"*En el fondo.*" *Siete días* (1969).

"Entrevista con Elvira Orphée." *Letras nuevas,* no. 12 (January–March 1975): 3–5.

Ferro, Helen. "*Uno,* en un libro de Elvira Orphée." *Clarín* (Buenos Aires), literary supplement (13 July 1961): 2.

Garfield, Evelyn Picon. "Desprendida a hachazos de la eternidad: Lo primordial en la obra de Elvira Orphée." *Journal of Latin American Lore* 5, no. 1 (1979): 3–23.

Gómez Paz, Julieta. "*Aire tan dulce.*" *La prensa* (3 September 1967).

"Hijas, libros y gatos." *Análisis,* no. 425 (6–12 May 1969): 51.

Justo, Luis. "Elvira Orphée y sus novelas." *Sur,* no. 315 (November–December 1968): 88–89.

"La seducción de lo prohibido en un sagaz libro de Elvira Orphée." *La Opinión.* (23 July 1973).

Loubet, Jorgelina. "Lo cotidiano, el fulgor y el signo en la obra de actuales escritoras argentinas." *Zona Franca* (Caracas) 3, no. 20 (September–October 1980): 7–23.

M. E. V. "Entre demencias y ángeles." *La Nación* (14 June 1978).

Peltzer, Federico. "Tres mujeres solas en la novelística argentina." *Sur* (1974).

R. C. de B. "*Dos veranos* de Elvira Orphée." *El Mundo* (2 September 1956).

Review of *Aire tan dulce. Papel Literario de Caracas* (9 July 1978).

"Su demonio preferido." *La Nación* (17 June 1973).

"Tres formas de soledad y una notable novelista." *Panorama* (April 1967).

Valenzuela, Luisa. "La belleza que lastima." *La Nación* (3 August 1969).

Marta Traba

Fiction

Historia natural de la alegría. Buenos Aires, 1951.

Las ceremonias del verano. 1st ed. Havana, Cuba, 1966. 2nd ed. Buenos Aires, Argentina, 1967.

Los laberintos insolados. Spain, 1967.

Pasó así. Montevideo, 1968.

La jugada del sexto día. Santiago, Chile, 1969.

Homérica Latina. Bogotá, Colombia, 1979.

Conversación al sur. Mexico, 1981.

En cualquier lugas. Bogotá, Colombia, 1984.

Marta Traba, selección de textos. Bogotá, Colombia, 1984.

Art History and Art Criticism

Art in Colombia. Washington, D.C., 1959.

La pintura nueva en Latinoamérica. Bogotá, 1961.

Seis artistas contemporáneos colombianos. Bogotá, 1963.

Los cuatro monstruos cardinales. Mexico, 1963.

Historia abierta del arte colombiano. Cali, 1968.

Propuesta polémica sobre el arte puertorriqueño. San Juan, Puerto Rico, 1971.

La rebelión de los santos. San Juan, Puerto Rico, 1971.

En el umbral del arte moderno. San Juan, Puerto Rico, 1972.

Dos décadas vulnerables. Mexico, 1973.

Mirar en Caracas. Caracas, Venezuela, 1974.

Los signos de vida. Mexico, 1976.

La zona del silencio. Mexico, 1976.

Los muebles de Beatriz González. Bogotá, 1977.

Los grabados de Roda. Bogotá, 1977.

Mirar en Bogotá. Bogotá, 1977.

Short Works

"Hipótesis sobre una escritura diferente." *FEM* 6, no. 2 (February–March 1982).

Articles published in *El Tiempo, Semana, La Nueva Prensa,* and *Eco* (Bogotá); *Marcha* (Montevideo); *El Nacional, Ultimas Noticias,* and *El Universal* (Caracas); and *Sábado* (Mexico).

Secondary Sources

Calderón, Alfonso. "Laberintos de verano." *Ercilla* 32, no. 1,645 (14 December 1966): 35.

———. "La gente por dentro." *Ercilla* 34, no. 1,732 (28 August 1968): 51.

Chevigny, Bell. "Ambushing the Will to Ignorance: Elvira Orphée's *La última conquista de el Angel* and Marta Traba's *Conversación al sur.*" In *El cono sur: Dinámica y dimensiones de su literatura,* edited by Rose S. Minc. Upper Montclair, N.J., 1985, pp. 98–104.

———. "Angel Rama and Marta Traba: A Latin American Odyssey Ends." *Nation,* February 4, 1984, pp. 126–28.

Cobo Borda, Juan Gustavo. "Spanish American Fiction, 1981." *Center for Inter-American Relations Review* 31 (April 1982): 83–87.

García Ramos, Reinaldo. "La novelista y sus veranos." *Casa de las Américas* 6, nos. 36–37 (May–August 1966): 190–94.

Grossman, Edith. "In Memoriam." *Center for Inter-American Relations Review* 32 (1984): 8.

Mejía Duque, Jaime. "*Las ceremonias del verano.*" *Boletín Cultural y Bibliográfico* (Bogotá) 10, no. 4 (1967): 867–70.

Moreira, Víctor. "Marta Traba, una muñeca de trapo que dice cosas terribles." *La Nación* (25 August 1969): 16–17.

Rama, Angel. "La persecución de Marta Traba." *Punto Final* 1, no. 18 (December 1966): 20–21.

Sola, María. "*Conversación al Sur,* novela para no olvidar." *Sin nombre* (San Juan, Puerto Rico) 12, no. 4 (July–September 1982): 64–71.

Waller, Claudia J. "Light and Darkness in Marta Traba's *Los laberintos insolados.*" *Romance Notes* 14 (1972): 262–68.

Luisa Valenzuela

Fiction

Hay que sonreír. Buenos Aires, 1966; appeared as *Clara: Thirteen Short Stories and a Novel,* translated by Hortense Carpentier and J. Jorge Castello, New York/London, 1976. (Also includes *Los heréticos.*)

Los heréticos. Buenos Aires, 1967.

El gato eficaz. Mexico, 1972; two short stories from this appeared as "The First Feline Vision," translated by Evelyn Picon Garfield, *Antaeus,* no. 48 (Winter 1983): 75–78; and as "The Efficient Cat," translated by Evelyn Picon Garfield, *River Styx,* no. 14 (January 1984): 87–89.

Aquí pasan cosas raras. Buenos Aires, 1975; appeared as *Strange Things Happen Here,* translated by Helen Lane. New York/London, 1979. Short stories from this appeared as "The Best Shod" and "A Story about Greenery," *Ms* 7, no. 12 (June 1979): 60–61, and "Three Stories from *Strange Things Happen Here,*" *Center for Inter-American Relations Review* 24 (1979): 44–53. (Also includes *Como en la guerra.*)

Como en la guerra. Buenos Aires, 1977.

Libro que no muerde. Mexico, 1980.

"The Censors." *City 8* 1, no. 8 (New York) (1980): 66–68.

"Papito's Story." *City 8* 1, no. 8 (New York) (1980): 66–68. (Also included in *Donde viven las águilas.*)

Cambio de armas. Hanover, N.H., 1982.

Donde viven las águilas. Buenos Aires, 1983. A short story from this appeared as "Generous Impediments Float Down the River." In *Contemporary Women Authors of Latin America: New Translations,* edited by Doris Meyer and Margarite Fernández Olmos. New York, 1983, pp. 245–48.

Cola de lagartija. Buenos Aires, 1983; appeared as *The Lizard's Tail,* translated by Gregory Rabassa. New York, 1983.

"The Word that Milk Cow." *Contemporary Women Authors of Latin America: Introductory Essays,* edited by Doris Meyer and Margarite Fernández Olmos. New York, 1983, pp. 96–97.

Secondary Sources

Alonso, Trinidad. Review of *Como en la guerra. El Tribuno* (Salta) (7 August 1977).

Andrés, Alfredo, "Búsqueda, viaje y psicoanálisis." *La Opinión* 21 (September 1977): 18.

Castelar, Diana. *"Hay que sonreír." El Libro y Su Crónica* (1966): 65.

Cicco, Juan. "Laberintos del misterio." *La Nación* (28 August 1977).

Cook, Carole. *"Strange Things Happen Here:* Twenty-six Short Stories and a Novel." *Saturday Review* (23 June 1979): 80.

Cortázar, Julio. "Luisa Valenzuela." *Review: Latin American Literature and Arts,* no. 24 (1979): 44.

———. *"El gato eficaz." Bellas Artes* (21 January 1981).

Cruz, Jorge. *"Hay que sonreír." La Nación* (27 November 1966).

Dujovne Ortiz, Alicia. Review of *Como en la guerra. La Actualidad en el Arte* (November 1977).

E. E. "Juego hacia adentro: Un ducto para vencer la incomunicación." *El Día* (Montevideo) (20 August 1977).

Eichelbaum, Edmundo. *"Como en la guerra." Siete Días* (5 July 1977).

Fernández, Ruth. "Para el elogio. *Como en la guerra.*" *Clarín* (1 September 1977).

Fores, Ana M. "Luisa Valenzuela's Novels: A Totally Ambiguous Fluency." M.A. thesis, Montclair State College, 1981.

Garfield, Evelyn Picon. "Muerte-Metamorfosis-Modernidad: *El gato eficaz* de Luisa Valenzuela." *Insula* (Madrid), nos. 400–401 (March–April 1980): 17, 23.

Glantz, Margo. "*Como en la guerra.*" *Bellas Artes* (21 January 1981).

Grossman, Edith. "To Speak the Unspeakable." *Center for Inter-American Relations Review* 32 (1984): 33–34.

I. C. "*Como en la guerra.*" *Pluma y Pincel* (3 October 1977).

Ibargon, Saúl. "Todo libro debe morder: Luisa Valenzuela intenta moverle el piso al lector." *Excelsior* (12 August 1980).

Josephs, Allen. "Sorcerers and Despots." Review of *The Lizard's Tail. New York Times Book Review* (2 October 1983): 15, 26.

Katz, Jane. "I Was Always a Bit of a Rebel." In *Artists in Exile.* New York, 1982, pp. 59–70.

Luiselli, Alessandria. "Luisa Valenzuela: Desgarrada entre la poesía y la antropología." *Bellas Artes* (21 January 1981).

Magnarelli, Sharon. "Gatos, lenguaje, y mujeres en *El gato eficaz* de Luisa Valenzuela." *Revista Iberoamericana* 45, nos. 108–9 (July–December 1979): 603–11.

Martínez, Nelly. "*El gato eficaz* de Luisa Valenzuela: La productividad del texto." *Revista canadiense de estudios hispánicos* 4 (1979): 73–80.

Ponzano, Pablo G. "El mundo mágico de Luisa Valenzuela." *Córdoba* (16 July 1977): 5.

Review of *Hay que sonreír. Ficción* (January 1967).

Satinosky, Oscar. "La autora de *El gato eficaz* en un diálogo sobre su próxima obra." *La Opinión* (15 June 1977): 19.

Sersaty, Shelia R. Review of *Cambio de armas. Literatura Chilena: Creación y Crítica* 9, no. 1 (1985): 35.

"Una Ofelia frustrada, entre el amor y el mar." *Clarín* (27 October 1966): 4.

Zabala, Noemi. "*Hay que sonreír.*" *Comentario* (March–April 1967).

FURTHER READINGS

Alarcón, Norma, and Sylvia Kossnar. *Bibliography of Hispanic Women Writers.* Bloomington, Ind., 1980.

Anderson, Lola. "Mexican Women Journalists." *Bulletin of the Pan American Union* (Washington, D.C.) 68, no. 5 (1934): 315–20.

Araújo, Helena. "¿Cuál literatura femenina?" *El Espectador, Magazín Dominical* (Bogotá; 20 September 1981): 5–6.

Arzipe, Lourdes. "Interview with Carmen Naranjo." *Signs: Journal of Women in Culture and Society* 5: 98–110.

Birkemoe, Diane Solomon. "Contemporary Women Novelists of Argentina (1945–1967)." Ph.D. diss., University of Illinois, 1968.

Bullrich Palenque, Silvina. *La mujer argentina en la literatura.* Buenos Aires, 1972.

Carrera, Julieta. *La mujer en América escribe . . . Semblanzas.* Mexico, D.F., 1956.

Castedo-Ellerman, Elena. "Feminism or Femininity? Six Women Writers Answer." *Américas* 30, no. 1 (October 1978): 19–24.

Castellanos, Rosario. *Mujer que sabe latín . . .* Mexico, D.F., 1973.

Chaney, Elsa M. *Supermadre: Women in Politics in Latin America.* Austin, 1979.

Chase, Kathleen. "Latin American Women Writers: Their Present Position." *Books Abroad* 33 (1959): 150–51.

Class, Bradley Mellon. "Fictional Treatment of Politics by Argentine Female Novelists." Ph.D. diss., University of New Mexico, 1974.

Correas de Zapata, Celia. "One Hundred Years of Women Writers in Latin America." *Latin American Literary Review* 3 (1975): 7–16.

———. *Detrás de la reja*. Caracas, 1980.

Cortina, Lynn Ellen Rice. *South American Women Writers: A Bibliographical Research Checklist*. New York, 1983.

Corvalán, Graciela N. V. *Latin American Women Writers in English Translation: A Bibliography*. Los Angeles, 1980.

Cuarto Congreso Interamericano de Escritoras en México. *La Semana de Bellas Artes,* no. 178 (April 1981); *La Semana de Bellas Artes,* no. 190 (22 July 1981); *Los Universitarios,* no. 187 (July 1981).

Cypess, Sandra Messinger. "¿Quién ha oído hablar de ellas? Una revisión de las dramaturgas mexicanas." *Texto Crítico* 10 (1978): 55–64.

Eco (Bogotá) no. 248 (June 1982).

Elu de Leñero, María del Carmen. *La mujer en América Latina*. 2 vols. Mexico City, 1975.

Figueira, Gastón. "Daughters of the Muse." *Américas* 2, no. 11 (1950): 28–31, 39.

Fox-Lockert, Lucía. *Women Novelists in Spain and Spanish America*. Metuchen, N.J., 1979.

Gardener, Mary A. "Press Woman's Role in Chile." *Matrix* 528: 6–7, 22–23.

Giusti, Roberto F. "Letras argentinas: La protesta de las mujeres." *Nosotros* 3, no. 10 (1937): 87–93.

Guillon Barrett, Yvonne. "The Poetess's Rejoinder to the Very Illustrious Sister, Sor Filotea de la Cruz and The Letter of Sor Filotea de la Cruz." Manuscript in progress.

Hahner, June E. *Women in Latin American History: Their Lives and Views*. Los Angeles, 1976.

Handelsman, Michael H. *Amazonas y artistas. Un estudio de la prosa de la mujer ecuatoriana*. 2 vols. Quito, Ecuador, 1978.

———. *Diez escritoras ecuatorianas y sus cuentos*. Quito, Ecuador, 1982.

Hoberman, Louisa S. "Hispanic American Women as Portrayed in the Historical Literature: Types or Archetypes?" *Revista Iberoamericana* 4 (1974): 136–47.

Holmes, Olive. "Women Pathbreakers of Chile." *National Business Woman* 23, no. 3 (1944): 68, 85–86.

Holt-Seeland, Inger. *Women of Cuba*. New York, 1982.

Jacobs, Sue-Ellen. *Women in Perspective: A Guide for Cross-Cultural Studies*. Chicago and Urbana, 1974.

Jiménez, Reynaldo L. "Cuban Women Writers and the Revolution: Toward an Assessment of Their Literary Contribution." *Folio* 11 (1978): 75–95.

Knaster, Meri. "Women in Latin America: The State of Research." *Latin American Research Review* 11, no. 1 (1976): 3–74.

———. *Women in Spanish America: An Annotated Bibliography from Pre-Conquest to Contemporary Times*. Boston, 1977.

Lavrín, Asunción, ed. *Latin American Women: Historical Perspectives*. Westport, Conn., 1978.

Lee, Muna. "Puerto Rican Women Writers: The Record of One Hundred Years." *Books Abroad* 8, no. 1 (1934): 7–10.

Leret de Matheus, María Gabriela. *La mujer, una incapaz como el demente y el niño (según las leyes latinoamericanas)*. Mexico, 1975.

Levine, Linda Gould, and Gloria Feiman Waldman. *Feminismo ante el Franquismo: Entrevistas con Feministas de España*. Miami, Fla., 1980.

Lewald, H. Ernest, trans. and ed. *The Web: Stories by Argentine Women.* Washington, D.C., 1983.

Lindstrom, Naomi. "Feminist Criticism of Latin American Literature." *Latin American Research Review* 15, no. 1 (1980): 151–59.

Los narradores ante el público. Mexico, D.F., 1966.

Luchting, Wolfgang. "¿Machismus moribundus?" *Mundo Nuevo* (Paris), no. 23 (May 1968): 61–67.

———. "¿Machismus moribundus? (II)." *Mundo Nuevo,* no. 24 (June 1968): 75–78.

Medina, José Toribio. *La literatura femenina en Chile. (Notas bibliográficas y en parte críticas).* Santiago, 1923.

Meyer, Doris. *Victoria Ocampo.* New York, 1979.

———, and Margarite Fernández Olmos. *Contemporary Women Authors of Latin America.* 2 vols. Brooklyn, 1983.

Miguel, María Esther de. "La mujer en su literatura y su responsabilidad como escritora." *Revista de la Universidad Nacional de Córdoba* (Córdoba, Argentina) 10, nos. 1/2 (1969): 321–37.

Miller, Beth. *Mujeres en la literatura.* Mexico, 1978.

———, ed. *Women in Hispanic Literature: Icons and Fallen Idols.* Berkeley, California, 1983.

———, and Alfonso González, eds. *26 autoras del México actual.* Mexico, 1978.

Miller, Yvette E., and Charles M. Tatum, eds. *Latin American Women Writers: Yesterday and Today.* Pittsburgh, 1977.

Miranda, Marta Elba. *Mujeres chilenas.* Santiago, 1940.

Mora, Gabriela. "Hispanic American Fiction and Drama Written by Women: Suggested Readings." Chapter in *Female Studies IX: Teaching about Women in the Foreign Languages.* New York, 1975, pp. 138–44.

———, and Karen S. Van Hooft, eds. *Theory and Practice of Feminist Literary Criticism.* Ypsilanti, Mich., 1982.

Moratorio, Arsinoe. *Mujeres del Uruguay.* Montevideo, 1946.

Mundo Nuevo, no. 46 (April 1970): 14–50.

Munk Benton, Gabriele von. "Women Writers of Contemporary Mexico." *Books Abroad* 33, no. 1 (1959): 15–19.

Muraro, Rose Marie. *Women in Latin America: Phases of Integration.* Program in Latin American Studies Occasional Papers Series, no. 6. University of Massachusetts at Amherst, 1977.

Nash, June, and Helen Icken Safa. *Sex and Class in Latin America. Women's Perspectives on Politics, Economics and Family in the Third World.* Brooklyn, 1980.

Nuceti-Sardi, José, and Lucila L. De Pérez Díaz. "Women in Venezuelan Literature." *Bulletin of the Pan American Union* (Washington, D.C.) 63, no. 5 (1929): 467–74.

Ocampo de Gómez, Aurora M., and Ernesto Prado Velázquez. *Diccionario de escritores mexicanos.* Mexico, D.F., 1967.

Paz, Octavio. *Sor Juana Inés de la Cruz o las trampas de la fe.* Mexico, 1982.

Paredes de Salazar, Elssa. *Diccionario biográfico de la mujer boliviana.* La Paz, 1965.

Peri Rossi, Cristina. "Literatura y mujer." *Eco* 42, no. 257 (March 1983): 498–506.

Pescatello, Ann, ed. *Female and Male in Latin America: Essays.* Pittsburgh, Pa., 1973.

———. Preface to "The Special Issue in Perspective: The Hispanic Caribbean Woman and the Literary Media." *Revista Interamericana/Interamerican Review* (Río Piedras, Puerto Rico) 4, no. 2 (1974): 131–35.

———. *Power and Pawn: The Female in Iberian Families, Societies and Cultures.* Westport, Conn., 1976.

Plá, Josefina. *Obra y aporte femeninos en la literatura nacional.* Asunción, Paraguay, 1976.

Poniatowska, Elena. "Mujer y literatura en América Latina." *Eco* 42 no. 257 (March 1983): 462–72.

Randall, Margaret. *Cuban Women Now: Interviews with Cuban Women.* Toronto, 1974.

———. *Women in Cuba—Twenty Years Later.* New York, 1981.

Redondo, Susana. "Proceso de la literatura femenina hispanoamericana." *Cuadernos* 6 (1954): 34–38.

Resnick, Margery, and Isabelle de Courtivron. *Women Writers in Translation: An Annotated Bibliography, 1945–1980.* New York, 1981.

Robles Suarez, Juana. *La mujer por la mujer.* Mexico, 1975.

Romero de Valle, Emilia, ed. *Mujeres de América.* Mexico, D.F., 1948.

Salgués Cargill, Maruxa. *La imagen de la mujer en las letras hispanoamericanas.* Jaen, 1975.

Sayers Peden, Margaret, trans. *A Woman of Genius: The Intellectual Autobiography of Sor Juana Inés de la Cruz.* Connecticut, 1981.

Shaw, Lee Roberts. "The Feminine Principle in a Masculine World: A Study of Contemporary Argentine Fiction by Women Writers, 1950–1970." Ph.D. diss., University of Tennessee, 1978.

Signs: Journal of Women in Culture and Society. Autumn 1979.

Silva Castro, Raúl. "Mujeres en las letras chilenas." *Cuadernos* 94 (1965): 75–80.

Sosa de Newton, Lily. *Diccionario biográfico de mujeres argentinas.* Buenos Aires, 1972.

"Special Edition: The Latin American Woman-Image and Reality." *Revista/Review Interamericana* 4, no. 2 (1974).

Stone, Elizabeth, ed. *Women and the Cuban Revolution: Speeches and Documents by Fidel Castro, Vilma Espín and Others.* New York, 1981.

Thurman, Judith. "Sister Juana: The Price of Genius." *Ms* 1, no. 10 (April 1973): 14–21.

Trenti Rocamora, J. Luis. *Grandes mujeres de América.* Buenos Aires, 1945.

Ugarte, Manuel. "Women Writers of South America." *Books Abroad* 5, no. 3 (1931) 238–41.

Urbano, Victoria, ed. *Five Women Writers of Costa Rica.* Texas, 1978.

Uribe Muñoz, Bernardo. *Mujeres de América.* Medellín, 1934.

Valdés, Nelson P. *A Bibliography on Cuban Women in the Twentieth Century.* Cuban Studies Newsletter, 4, no. 2 (June 1974).

Valenzuela, Victor, ed. *Grandes escritoras hispanoamericanas: poetisas y novelistas.* Bethlehem, Pa., 1974.

Walton, Whitney, Cathy Loeb, and Esther Stineman. *Current Sources on Women and Literature.* Madison, Wis., 1979.

Weeks, Elsie. "Great Chilean Women. IV. Literary Women." *Andean Monthly* (Santiago) 3, no. 7 (1940): 329–39.

Women in Latin American Literature: A Symposium. Program in Latin American Studies Occasional Papers Series, no. 10. University of Massachusetts at Amherst, 1979.

Young, Rinda Rebeca Stowell. "Six Representative Women Novelists of Mexico, 1960–69." Ph.D. diss., University of Illinois at Urbana-Champaign, 1975.

Zanelli López, Luisa. *Mujeres chilenas de letras. I.* Santiago, 1917.

Evelyn Picon Garfield is professor of Spanish at the University of Illinois at Urbana-Champaign. She received her A.B. from the University of Michigan, her M.A. from Washington University, St. Louis, and her Ph.D. from Rutgers University. She has previously taught at Wayne State University, Brown University, and Montclair State College. Dr. Garfield is the author of ¿Es Julio Cortázar un surrealista?, Julio Cortázar, Cortázar por Cortázar, *and numerous articles, and coauthor with I. A. Schulman of* "Las entrañas del vacío" : Ensayos sobre la modernidad hispanoamericana *and* Poesía modernista hispanoamericana y española (Antología).

The manuscript was prepared for publication by Anne M. G. Adamus. The book was designed by Don Ross. The typeface for the text is Times Roman, designed under the supervision of Stanley Morison about 1931. The typeface for the display is Caslon Modern.

Manufactured in the United States of America.